PASSENGERS NO MORE

PASSENGERS
NO
MORE

G. DANIELS & L. A. DENCH

LONDON

IAN ALLAN

*Published by Ian Allan Ltd., Shepperton, Middx. and
Printed in the United Kingdom by The Press at Coombelands Limited
Addlestone Weybridge Surrey*

PREFACE

When the early, primitive, petrol-driven motor cars first appeared towards the close of the nineteenth century, there were probably few who imagined that these slow and unreliable vehicles could ever become a serious challenge to the railways, the established mode of conveyance. But as the motor car and the omnibus gradually developed and the art of road making improved, it became evident that the time was coming when railways would no longer hold the virtual monopoly they had enjoyed for so long. The effect was first felt during and following the first world war and by the 1920's the matter was beginning to assume serious proportions. As yet no real threat had appeared to long distance journeys, for which rail travel was, and generally speaking still is, the ideal medium, whilst air transport was only in its infancy. Nevertheless serious inroads were already being made on the short distance traffic, this being particularly the case in country districts. Here the railway station was often situated at a considerable distance from the town or village which it served. The trains were often infrequent or awkwardly timed and sometimes involved tiresome waits at a junction for connections. The omnibus, on the other hand, was able to pick up its passengers almost on their doorsteps and deposit them in the centre of the neighbouring town. Services could be more frequent and above all it was possible to charge considerably lower fares owing to lower costs of operation. This was chiefly due to the fact that the omnibus proprietor had his track—the public roads—already there and maintained by the country at large; a railway has to pay for its own track.

Admittedly the railways were far too slow in taking steps to combat the threat of road competition but where the station was a mile or two from the village it was built to serve, little could be done. The number of private cars in Britain has multiplied considerably over the last few years, and even more conveniently situated stations have lost nearly all their passengers.

At the time of writing the first effects of the "Beeching Report" are just being felt. If and when all of this has been implemented the light railway and country branch line which most of us know will have disappeared from the scene.

Whilst we have listed every branch line and station known to us to have had a regular, advertised passenger service and which closed between 1919 and 1963, a period of 45 years, unfortunately only a mere fraction can be illustrated here. Photographs used have been individually credited. We are indebted to H. C. Casserley's book "Service Suspended" which has supplied essential material (suitably brought up-to-date) for use in this volume. Acknowledgements are due also to Messrs. E. Wilmshurst, D. A. Lawrence, R. W. Patterson and others for their help in the preparation of "Passengers No More".

Brighton

G. DANIELS
L. A. DENCH

RAILWAY COMPANY ABBREVIATIONS

AJ	—Axholme Joint (LY&NE).	HB	—Hull & Barnsley.
Ash.	—Ashover Light.	HJ	—Halesowen J. (GW and Mid.)
BC	—Bishop's Castle.	HR	—Highland.
BJ	—Birkenhead Joint (GW and LNW).	IMR	—Isle of Man.
		IWC	—Isle of Wight Central.
BL	—Brackenhill Light.	IWR	—Isle of Wight.
BM	—Brecon & Merthyr.	KE	—Knott End.
BPGV	—Burry Port & Gwendraeth Valley.	KES	—Kent & East Sussex Light.
		L&M	—Leek and Manifold.
BRY	—Barry.	LB	—Lynton & Barnstaple.
Cal.	—Caledonian.	LBSC	—London, Brighton & South Coast.
Cam.	—Cambrian.		
Car.	—Cardiff.	LMR	—London Midland Region.
CKP	—Cockermouth, Keswick & Penrith.	LMS	—London Midland & Scottish.
		LNE	—London & North Eastern.
CL	—Corringham Light.	LNW	—London & North Western.
CLC	—Cheshire Lines Committee (GC, GN and Midland).	LOR	—Liverpool Overhead Railway.
		LPTB	—London Passenger Transport Board.
CM	—Campletown & Machrihanish Light.		
		LSW	—London & South Western.
CMDP	—Cleobury Mortimer & Ditton Priors Light.	LTE	—London Transport Executive.
		LUJ	—Lancashire & Yorkshire and Lancashire Union Joint (LNW and LY).
CO	—Croydon & Oxted Joint (LBSC and SEC).		
Cor.	—Corris.	LY	—Lancashire and Yorkshire.
CVH	—Colne Valley & Halstead.	Met.	—Metropolitan.
CWJ	—Cleator & Workington Junction.	M&C	—Maryport & Carlisle.
		MD	—Metropolitan & District Joint.
D&A	—Dundee & Arbroath Joint (Cal. and NB).	MGC	—Metropolitan & Great Central Joint.
		MGN	—Midland & Great Northern Joint (GN and Midland).
DV	—Dearne Valley.		
DVL	—Derwent Valley Light.	Mid.	—Midland.
Eas.	—Easingwold.	MJ	—Methley Joint (GN, LY and NE).
ECH	—Easton & Church Hope (GW and LSW).		
		MNR	—Manx Northern.
EK	—East Kent.	MSL	—Mid Suffolk Light.
ER	—Eastern Region.	MSW	—Midland & South Western Junction.
Fest.	—Festiniog.		
FMJ	—Furness & Midland Joint.	Mum.	—Swansea & Mumbles.
Fur.	—Furness.	N&B	—Neath & Brecon.
FYN	—Freshwater, Yarmouth and Newport.	NB	—North British.
		NE	—North Eastern Railway.
GBK	—Glasgow, Barrhead & Kilmarnock Joint (Cal. and GSW).	NER	—North Eastern Region.
		NL	—North London.
GC	—Great Central.	NS	—North Staffordshire.
GE	—Great Eastern.	NSJ	—Norfolk & Suffolk Joint (GE and MGN).
GN	—Great Northern.		
GNS	—Great North of Scotland.	NSL	—North Sunderland Light.
G&P	—Glasgow & Paisley Joint (Cal. and GSW).	NSW	—North & South Western Junction (LNW, Mid and NL).
GSW	—Glasgow & South Western.	NUJ	—North Union Joint (LNW and LY).
GVT	—Glyn Valley Tramway.		
GW	—Great Western.		

NV	—Nidd Valley.
NWNG	—North Wales Narrow Gauge.
OAGB	—Oldham, Ashton-under-Lyne & Guide Bridge (GC and LNW).
QYM	—Quaker's Yard & Merthyr Joint (GW and Rhymney).
PL	—Preston & Longridge Joint (LNW and LY).
PLA	—Port of London Authority.
PT	—Port Talbot Railway and Docks.
PPW	—Portpatrick and Wigtownshire Joint (Cal., Mid., GSW and LNW).
PWY	—Preston & Wyre (LNW and LY).
RCT	—Rye & Camber Tramway.
Rhy.	—Rhymney.
RSB	—Rhondda & Swansea Bay.
ScR	—Scottish Region.
SD	—Somerset & Dorset Joint Committee (LSW and Midland).
SEC	—South Eastern & Chatham.
S&H	—Shrewsbury & Hereford Joint (GW and LNW).
SHT	—Sand Hutton Light.
SK	—Swinton & Knottingley (Midland and NE).
S&M	—Shropshire & Montgomeryshire Light.
SMJ	—Stratford-on-Avon & Midland Junction.
SR	—Southern Region.
SRy	—Southern Railway.
SSM	—South Shields, Marsden & Whitburn Colliery.

ST	—Hundred of Manhood and Selsey Tramway.
SVW	—Severn & Wye Joint (GW and Midland).
SWD	—Southwold.
SWM	—South Wales Mineral.
SWP	—Shrewsbury & Welshpool Joint (GW and LNW).
SWT	—South Wales Transport.
SYJ	—South Yorkshire Joint (GC, GN, LY, Midland and NE).
Tal.	—Talyllyn.
THJ	—Tottenham & Hampstead Junction (GE and Midland).
TV	—Taff Vale.
VR	—Vale of Rheidol (Cambrian).
VT	—Vale of Towy Joint (GW and LNW).
WCE	—Whitehaven, Cleator & Egremont Joint (Furness and LNW).
WCP	—Weston, Clevedon and Portishead.
WH	—Welsh Highland.
Wir.	—Wirral.
W&L	—Welshpool & Llanfair Light (Cambrian).
WL	—West London (GW and LNW).
WLE	—West London Extension (GW, LNW, LBSC and LSW).
WP	—Weymouth & Portland Joint (GW and LSW).
WR	—Western Region.
WRG	—West Riding and Grimsby Joint (GC and GN).
WT	—Wantage Tramway.

The last day of the Hayling Island branch service. Class A1X 0-6-0T No. 32670 crosses Langston Bridge with the 4.35 p.m. from Havant to Hayling Island on November 2, 1963.

[B. STEPHENSON

ABOVE: *Cliddesden station on the Basingstoke—Alton branch, photographed in 1931. This station was later used for the setting of the Will Hay film "Oh Mr. Porter" for which purpose it was re-named Buggleskelly.* [H. C. CASSERLEY

BELOW: *The Ebbw Vale branch platforms at Aberbeeg.* [G. DANIELS

INTRODUCTION

Regular advertised passenger services only, in Great Britain, are shown in this publication, although in some cases workmen's trains and occasional excursions may still be run.

Entries in bold type show both ends of a stretch of line at time of closure. In the case of a branch line having a terminal station, this is given preference over the junction. The actual track involved is deemed to be between these points except where such physical junctions are outside normal station limits and/or bear a different name to the station(s) concerned, when these are quoted by lower case lettering in parenthesis e.g. **Aberayron—Lampeter** (Aberayron Jn). *Italics* are used to help locate track closures where no actual station is involved e.g. *Arthington* **(West Junction—North Junction).**

Individual station entries are those closures on lines which continued to be used by passenger trains; junction stations closed with their relevant branch lines, are listed separately e.g. Moat Lane Junction.

Complete consistency, with regard to "curves" and running connections, in a work of this kind is almost impossible but those which have been included had a direct association with the passenger service in operation at the time of withdrawal.

The railway company (or regional administration, if after 1st January, 1948) at time of closure is shown, followed by the ownership immediately prior to the grouping of 1923. When two regions were involved in the closure of a section of line, both have been shown except where the junction station only is in a different one; in such instances only the region responsible for the line concerned has been named. Preliminary amalgamations during the earlier part of that decade have been ignored, e.g. LY with LNW. A few lines and stations, whilst nominally independent, are accredited to their parent Working company or Committee e.g. London & Blackwall. Simultaneous complete closure of a line is denoted by an asterisk (*); when this occurred subsequently a footnote is added. Only the more significant temporary closures have been included. London Transport tube lines have not been catered for.

The map reference quoted at the end of each entry refers to the Ian Allan "Pre-Grouping Gazetter." Abbreviations used in this publication are as follows:-

✠—Not indicated on map.	RN—Renamed.
Cl.—Closed.	RO—Reopened.
(P)—Passengers	TC—Temporarily closed.

PC—Closed permanently to passengers at date shown.

ø—Closed to all traffic, date unknown.

NARROW GAUGE RAILWAYS

Station or line	Owner-ship at Closure	Former Owner-ship	Gauge	Date Closed			Map Ref	Note
Aberllefeni—Machynlleth	GW	Cor.	2′ 3″	1	1	31	14B5	2
Ashover—Clay Cross	Ash.	Ash.	60 cm	14	9	36	16B5✠	3
Ballabeg	IMR	IMR	3′	4	10	48	23C2	
Bossall—Warthill	SHT	SHT	1′ 6″	7	7	30	21C5✠	4
Boston Lodge Halt	Fest.	Fest.	1′ 11½″	28	9	36	19F2	5
Camber Sands—Rye	RCT	RCT	3′	4	9	39	6E4	6
Campbeltown—Machrihanish	CM	CM	2′ 3″	–	9	31	29F1	7
Devils Bridge—Aberystwyth	GW	VR	1′ 11½″	31	8	39	14C5	8
Dinas Junction—Portmadoc	WH	WH	1′ 11½″	28	9	36	19E2	9
Duffws—Portmadoc (Harbour):								
Duffws—Blaenau Festiniog	Fest.	Fest.	1′ 11½″	1	6	31	19F3	10
Blaenau Festiniog— Portmadoc (Harbour)	Fest.	Fest.	1′ 11½″	16	9	39	19F2	11
Foxdale—St. Johns	IMR	MNR	3′	16	5	40	23B2	12
Glynceiriog—Chirk	GVT	GVT	2′ 4½″	6	4	33	20F5	13
Hulme End—Waterhouses	LMS	L&M	2′ 6″	29	9	35	15B5	*
Lezayre	IMR	MNR	3′	2	10	61	23A3	
Llanfair Caereinion—Welshpool	GW	W&L	2′ 6″	9	2	31	14B3	14
Lynton—Barnstaple Town	SRy	LB	1′ 11½″	29	9	35	7E4	*
Peel Road	IMR	MNR	3′	2	6	52	23B2	
Southwold—Halesworth	SWD	SWD	3′	12	4	29	12B1	*
Stony Stratford—Wolverton	LMS	LNW	3′ 6″	4	5	26	10C2✠	*
Union Mills	IMR	IMR	3′	22	5	61	23B2	

2. *21.8.48. **3.** *31.3.50. **4.** *24.10.32. **5.** RO 23.7.55 with line (see note 11). **6.** Transferred to WD –.–.40; *–.–.45. **7.** *–.11.32. **8.** Ran in summer only from 1932. Cl. to freight 26.9.37. RO for passengers summer only 23.7.45. **9.** Dinas Jn—Beddgelert as NWNGR Cl. 1.11.16, RO 31.7.22, ext to Portmadoc 1.6.23; whole *21.6.37, incl. Bryngwyn—Tryfan Jn (Cl.P. 1.1.14). **10.** Cl. 1.1.23, RO 1.1.25, *2.8.46. **11.** *2.8.46. RO by FRS Portmadoc—Boston Lodge 23.7.55, to Minffordd 19.5.56, to Penrhyndeudraeth 30.3.57, to Tan-y-Bwlch 5.4.58. **12.** Not officially closed but no trains have run since this date. **13.** *6.7.35. **14.** *5.11.56; RO by W&LPS Llanfair Caereinion—Castle Caereinion 6.4.63, Castle Caereinion —Sylfaen 6.6.64.

Station or line	Ownership at Closure	Pre-Group Company	Date Closed	Map Ref	Note
Abbey Holme—Kirtlebridge:					
Abbey Holme—Annan					
(Shaw Hill)	Cal.	Cal.	1 9 21	26C2	20
Annan (Shaw Hill)—Kirtle-					
bridge	LMS	Cal.	27 4 31	26B2	20
Abbey Holme—Brayton	LMS	Cal.	13 2 33	26C2	*
Abbotsbury—Upwey Junction	SR	GW	1 12 52	3F2	2
Abbotsford Ferry	LNE	NB	5 1 31	30E1	
Abbots Ripton	ER	GN	15 9 58	11B2	
Aber	LMR	LNW	12 9 60	19D3	
Aberayron—Lampeter					
(Aberayron Jn)	WR	GW	7 5 51	13D4	3
Abercwmboi Halt	WR	TV	2 4 56	43C2	
Abercynon (Stormstown Jn)—					
Ynysybwl (New Road) Halt					
(Windsor Passing Sdg)	WR	TV	28 7 52	43D3	
Aberfoyle—Kirkintilloch	ScR	NB	1 10 51	29A4	4
Abergavenny Junction	WR	GW	9 6 58	43A1	
Abergavenny Jn—Merthyr					
(Morlais Tunnel Jn)	WR	LNW	6 1 58	43A1	5
Abergwynfi—Cymmer Afan					
(Gelli)	WR	GW	13 6 60	43D3	
Aberthaw—Llantrisant:					
Aberthaw—Cowbridge	GW	TV	5 5 30	43C5	6
Cowbridge—Llantrisant	WR	TV	26 11 51	43D4	
Abingdon—Radley	WR	GW	9 9 63	10F4	
Aby	ER	GN	11 9 61	17A3	
Acton Bridge (Hartford Jn					
(LNW))—Hartford &					
Greenbank (Hartford Jn (CLC))	LMS	LNW	— 6 47	15A2	
Admiralty Pier—Holyhead	LMS	LNW	31 3 35	19B2	
Aintree—Marsh Lane	LMR	LY	2 4 51	45F3	
Airdrie (East)—Whifflet					
(Upper)	LMS	Cal.	3 5 43	44B4	
Airdrie (East)—Newhouse	LMS	Cal.	1 12 30	44B4	31
Airdrie (South)—Ratho					
(Bathgate Jn)	ScR	NB	9 1 56	30C4	
Airth	ScR	Cal.	20 9 54	30A5	
Akeman Street	LNE	GC	7 7 30	10E3	
Albert Road Halt	SRy	LSW	13 1 47	1D5✠	
Albion	LMR	LNW	1 2 60	13B2	
Alcester—Bearley (North Jn)	GW	GW	25 9 39	9B5	7
Alexandra Dock—Spellow					
(Bootle Jn)	LMR	LNW	26 2 49	45F3	8
Alexandra Pal.—Finsbury Pk.	ER	GN	5 7 54	40A5	9
Alford Halt	WR	GW	10 9 62	8F1	
Alford—Kintore	ScR	GNS	2 1 50	37F2	
Algarkirk & Sutterton	ER	GN	11 9 61	17D2	
Allendale—Hexham					
(Border Counties Jn)	LNE	NE	22 9 30	27C3	10
Allhallows-on-Sea—Stoke					
Junction Halt	SR	—	4 12 61	6B5✠	*

Station or line	Ownership at Closure	Pre-Group Company	Date Closed			Map Ref	Note
Alloa (Kincardine Jn)— **Dunfermline** (Charlestown Jn) via Culross	LNE	NB	7	7	30	30A4	
All Stretton Halt	WR	S&H	9	6	58	14B1✠	
Alne	NER	NE	5	5	58	21B4	
Alness	ScR	HR	13	6	60	36C5	
Alnwick—Coldstream	LNE	NE	22	9	30	31F4	12
Alsager Road (East Jn)—**Keele**	LMS	NS	27	4	31	15C3	13
Altcar & Hillhouse—Meols Cop:							
Altcar & Hillhouse (Hillhouse Jn)—**Downholland**	LMS	LY	15	11	26	45F2	14
Downholland—Meols Cop (Butts Lane Jn)	LMS	LY	26	9	38	45F2	14
Althorp Park	LMR	LNW	13	6	60	10B3	
Alton (Butts Jn)—**Basingstoke**	SRy	LSW	12	9	32	4C2	15
Alton—Fareham (Knowle Jn)	SR	LSW	7	2	55	4D2	16
Alva—Cambus	ScR	NB	1	11	54	30A5	28
Alverthorpe	NER	GN	5	4	54	42C3	
Alyth—Alyth Junction	ScR	Cal.	2	7	51	34D5	
Alyth Junction—Dundee (West) (Ninewells Jn)	ScR	Cal.	10	1	55	34D5	17
Ambergate (Crich Jn)—**Pye Bridge** (Riddings Jn)	LMS	Mid.	16	6	47	41E2	
Amble—Chevington (Amble Branch Jn)	LNE	NE	7	7	30	31F5	
Ampleforth	NER	NE	5	6	50	21A5	
Ampthill	LMR	Mid.	4	5	59	10C1	
Anderston Cross	ScR	Cal.	3	8	59	44E4	
Andover Junction— Andoversford Junction	SR/WR	MSW	11	9	61	4B5	19
Andoversford & Dowdeswell	GW	MSW	1	4	27	9D4	
Angel Road—Lower Edmonton (Low Level)	LNE	GE	7	9	39	5A3	
Annbank—Mauchline	LMS	GSW	4	1	43	29E4	
Annesley	LMR	Mid.	6	4	53	41E4	
Annitsford	NER	NE	15	9	58	27B5	
Arbroath (St. Vigean's Jn)— **Forfar** (Guthrie Jn)	ScR	Cal.	5	12	55	34D3	21
Ardler	ScR	Cal.	11	6	56	34D5	
Ardley Halt	WR	GW	7	1	63	10D4	
Ardrossan—Neilston (High):							
Ardrossan (Montgomery Pier) (Stevenston No. 1)— **Uplawmoor**	LMS	Cal.	4	7	32	29D3	29
Uplawmoor—Neilston (High)	ScR	Cal.	2	4	62	44G2	
Arkholme	LMR	FMJ	12	9	60	24B2	
Arkwright Street	LMR	GC	4	3	63	41G4	
Arksey	ER	GN	4	8	52	21F5	
Arlesey & Henlow	ER	GN	5	1	59	11D2	
Arley & Fillongley	LMR	Mid.	7	11	60	16G5	

Station or line	Ownership at Closure	Pre-Group Company	Date Closed	Map Ref	Note
Armitage	LMR	LNW	13 6 60	15E5	
Arnside—Oxenholme (Hincaster Jn)	LMR	Fur.	1 3 53	24A3	22
Arthington **(West Junction— North Junction)**	NER	NE	25 2 57	21D3	
Asfordby	LMR	Mid.	2 4 51	16E3	
Ashburton—Totnes	WR	GW	3 11 58	2C4	18
Ashby-de-la-Zouch— Peartree & Normanton (Melbourne Jn)	LMS	Mid.	22 9 30	16E5	32
Ashchurch—Great Malvern: Ashchurch—Upton-on- Severn	WR	Mid.	14 8 61	9C3	27
Upton-on-Severn—Great Malvern (Malvern Jn)	WR	Mid.	1 12 52	9C3	*
Ashchurch—Redditch	WR	Mid.	17 6 63	9D3	24
Ashley & Weston	LMR	LNW	18 6 51	16F2	
Ashton-Under-Lyne (Park Parade)	LMR	GC	5 11 56	21A2	
Aspatria—Wigton: Aspatria—Mealsgate	LMS	M&C	22 9 30	26D2	ø
Mealsgate—Wigton (Aikbank Jn)	M&C	M&C	1 8 21	26D2	ø
Astley	LMR	LNW	7 5 56	45C3	
Ashton-by-Stone	LMS	NS	6 1 47	15D3	
Attercliffe	LNE	GC	26 9 27	42G2	
Auchinleck—Cronberry	ScR	GSW	4 7 50	29F5	
Auchterader	ScR	Cal.	11 6 56	33F4	
Audenshaw	LMR	LNW	25 9 50	21A2	
Auldbar Road	ScR	Cal.	11 6 56	34D3	
Auldearn	ScR	HR	6 6 60	36D3	
Auldgirth	ScR	GSW	3 11 52	26A4	
Authorpe	ER	GN	11 9 61	17A3	
Awre (for Blakeney)	WR	GW	10 8 59	8A1	
Aycliffe	NER	NE	2 3 53	28E5	
Aylesbury (High Street)— Cheddington	LMR	LNW	2 2 53	10E2	23
Aynho Park Platform	LMR	GW	7 1 63	10D4	
Ayr—Girvan (via Maidens): **Ayr** (Alloway Jn)— **Turnberry**	LMS	GSW	1 12 30	29F3	25
Turnberry—Girvan	LMS	GSW	3 3 42	29F3	26
Ayr (Hawkhill Jn)— **Muirkirk** via Drongan	ScR	GSW	10 9 51	29F3	30
Ayton	ScR	NB	5 2 62	31C3	

2. Abbotsbury—Upwey*, Upwey—Upwey Jn* 1.1.62. **3.** PC. TC 12.2.51. **4.** Aberfoyle— Campsie Glen* 5.10.59. **5.** Clydach—Beaufort Brickworks sidings and Nantybwch—Morlais Tunnel Jn were closed to goods traffic on 22.11.54. Abergavenny (Brecon Road)—Clydach*. Beaufort Brickworks—Nantybwch* 2.11.59. **6.** Cl. 4.5.26, RO 11.7.27. *1.11.32. **7.** *1.3.51. Workmen's trains continued between Birmingham and Great Alne until 3.7.44. **8.** PC. TC 31.5.48. **9.** Cl. 29.10.51, RO 7.1.52. Muswell Hill—Alexandra Palace* 5.7.54, Highgate— Muswell Hill* 18.5.57. **10.** *20.11.50. **12.** Ilderton—Wooler* –.8.48 (Floods). Alnwick—

Ilderton *2.3.53. **13.** *7.1.63. **14.** Downholland formerly Barton. Hillhouse Jn—Shirdley Hill *21.1.52. **15.** Cl. 1.1.17, RO 18.8.24.* 1.6.36. **16.** Farringdon—Droxford*. Droxford —Knowle Jn* 30.4.62. **17.** Auchterhouse—Newtyle Jn with branch to Newtyle Goods* 5.5.58. **18.** *10.9.62. **19. Grafton** (South Jn)—**Marlborough** via Savernake (H.L.) Cl. 15.9.58 (P), *22.6.59. Ludgershall—Savernake (Wolfhall Jn), Marlborough—Swindon (Town), Cirencester (Watermoor)—Andoversford & Dowdeswell*. Andoversford & Dowdeswell—Andoversford Jn* 15.10.62. Cirencester (Watermoor)—Moredon Power Stn *1.4.64; Swindon (Town)—Rushey Platt Jn *11.5.64. **20.** Annan (Shawhill)—Annan (G.S.W.) *28.2.55. **21.** Colliston—St. Vigean's Jn*. **22.** PC. TC 4.5.42. Sandside— Hincaster Jn* 9.9.63. **23.** *2.12.63. **24.** Evesham—Alcester*. Trains withdrawn between Evesham and Redditch 1.10.62 due to condition of track. Substitute bus service provided. Evesham—Ashchurch *9.9.63. **25.** Heads of Ayr—Turnberry *28.2.55. A new station for Butlin's Holiday Camp was opened at Heads of Ayr on 17.5.47, served in summer only. **26.** *28.2.55. **27.** Upton-on-Severn—Tewkesbury *1.7.63. **28.** Alva-Menstrie *2.3.64. **29.** Stevenston (jn with new spur)—Kilwinning East* 16.6.47, Lugton (East Jn)—Giffen *-.12.50; Giffen—Kilwinningø. **30.** Skares (Dyke Branch Jn)—Cronberryø. **31.** Airdrie (East)—Chapelhallø. **32.** Ashby—New Lount Colliery Sdgsø.

Station or line	Ownership at Closure	Pre- Group Company	Date Closed		Map Ref	Note
Backney Halt	WR	—	12 2 62		9D1✠	
Bacup—Rochdale	LMS	LY	16 6 47		20A1	54
Baglan Jn.—Court Sart (Court Sart Jn)	GW	SWM	23 9 35		43F3	
Baildon	NER	Mid.	5 1 53		42A4	
Bailey Gate (Corfe Mullen Jn) **—Wimborne**	SD	SD	12 7 20		3F5	55
Bainton	NER	NE	20 9 54		22C4	
Baldersby	NER	NE	14 9 59		21A3	
Balderton	WR	GW	3 3 52		20E4	
Balloch—Stirling:						
Balloch (Forth & Clyde Jn)— **Balfron** (Gartness Jn)	LNE	NB	1 10 34		29B3	2
Gartness Jn—Buchlyvie	ScR	NB	1 10 51		29A4	70
Buchlyvie—Stirling	LNE	NB	1 10 34		29B4	49
Balne	NER	NE	15 9 58		21E5	
Balquhidder—Perth:						
Balquhidder—Comrie	ScR	Cal.	1 10 51		33F2	*
Crieff—Perth (Almond Valley Jn)	ScR	Cal.	1 10 51		33F3	
Bamfurlong	LMR	LNW	27 11 50		45D2	
Banavie Pier—Fort William (Banavie Jn)	LNE	NB	7 9 39		32C3	3
Banbury (Merton Street)— Buckingham	WR/LMR	LNW	2 1 61		10C4	53
Bangour—Uphall (Bangour Asylum Branch Jn)	NB	NB	4 5 21		30C4	
Bankfoot—Strathord	LMS	Cal.	13 4 31		33E5	
Bankhead	LNE	GNS	5 4 37		37F4	
Bannockburn	ScR	Cal.	2 1 50		30A5	
Bardney—Louth	ER	GN	5 11 51		17A2	4
Bardon Hill	LMR	Mid.	12 5 52		16E4	
Bardowie	LNE	NB	20 7 31		44E5	

Station or line	Ownership at Closure	Pre-Group Company	Date Closed			Map Ref	Note
Bargeddie	LNE	NB	24	9	27	44C4	
Barkston	ER	GN	16	3	55	16C1	
Barnard Castle—Bishop Auckland	NER	NE	18	6	62	27E4	5
Barnard Castle—Penrith (Eden Valley Jn)	NER/LMR	NE	22	1	62	27E4	6
Barnby Moor & Sutton	ER	GN	7	11	49	16A3	
Barnsley **(Court House— Court House Junction)**	ER	Mid.	7	12	59	42E2	
Barnsley **(Court House —Junction with New Spur)**	ER	Mid.	19	4	60	42E2	*
Barnsley (Court House) (West Jn)—**Cudworth** (Sth Jn)	ER/NER	Mid.	9	6	58	42E2	63
Barnsley (Exchange)— Sheffield (Tinsley S. Jn)	ER	GC	7	12	53	42E2	
Barnstaple (Victoria Road)— Barnstaple South Loop Jn	SR	GW	13	6	60	7F3	*7
Barnstaple (Victoria Road)— Barnstaple East Loop Jn	SR	GW	13	6	60	7F3	*7
Barnton—Craigleith	ScR	Cal.	7	5	51	30B3	8
Barrow-in-Furness **(Dalton Jn.— Park South Jn)**	LMR	Fur.	15	9	58	24B5	
Barrow Hill	ER	Mid.	5	7	54	41B3	
Barrow (for Tarvin)	LMR	CLC	1	6	53	20D3	
Barton & Broughton	LMS	LNW	1	5	39	24D3	
Barton Hill	LNE	NE	22	9	30	22B5	
Barton Moss	LMS	LNW	23	9	29	45B3	
Barton & Walton	LMR	Mid.	5	8	58	15E5	
Baschurch	WR	GW	12	9	60	20G4	
Basford (North)—Netherfield & Colwick	LMR	GN	12	3	62	41F4	10
Basford (Vernon)	LMR	Mid.	4	1	60	41F4	
Basingstoke	GW	GW	1	1	32	4B2	
Bathgate (Upper) (Central Jn) **—Blackstone**	LNE	NB	1	5	30	30B4	
Bathgate (Upper) (Polkemmet Jn)**—Morningside**	LNE	NB	1	5	30	30B4	69
Batley—Beeston	NER	GN	29	10	51	42B3	9
Batley Carr	NER	GN	6	3	50	42C3	
Battersby—Picton	NER	NE	14	6	54	28F4	11
Battyeford	NER	LNW	5	10	53	42C4	
Bawtry	ER	GN	6	10	58	21G5	
Baxenden	LMR	LY	10	9	51	20A1	
Bay Horse	LMR	LNW	13	6	60	24C3	
Bealings	ER	GE	17	9	56	12D3	
Beamish	NER	NE	21	9	53	27C5	
Beanacre Halt	WR	GW	7	2	55	3A4	
Beauchief	ER	Mid.	2	1	61	41A2	
Beauly	ScR	HR	13	6	60	35D5	
Beccles—Tivetshall	ER	GE	5	1	53	18G2	12
Beccles—Yarmouth (South Town)	ER	GE	2	11	59	18F1	13

Station or line	Ownership at Closure	Pre-Group Company	Date Closed	Map Ref	Note
Beckingham	ER	GN&GE	2 11 59	22G5	
Beckton—Custom House	LNE	GE	7 9 40	40C1	
Bedford (Midland Road)— Hitchin	LMR	Mid.	1 1 62	11D1	59
Bedford (Midland Road) (Oakley Junction)—**Northampton (Bridge Street)**	LMR	Mid.	5 3 62	10C1	60
Bedlington—Morpeth	NER	NE	3 4 50	27A5	
Beeston	NER	GN	2 3 53	42B3	
Beighton	ER	GC	1 11 54	41A3	
Beith (Town)—Lugton	ScR	GBK	5 11 62	29D3	
Beith (North)	ScR	GSW	4 6 51	29D3	
Belgrave & Birstall	LMR	GC	4 3 63	16E3	
Bellahouston	ScR	GSW	20 9 54	44E3	
Bellahouston Park Halt	LMS	—	1 1 39	44E3✠	
Bell Busk	LMR	Mid.	4 5 59	21C1	
Bembridge—Brading	SR	IWR	21 9 53	4F2	*
Bengeworth	WR	Mid.	8 6 53	9C4	
Beningborough	NER	NE	15 9 58	21C4	
Bensham	NER	NE	5 4 54	27C5	
Berrington & Eye	WR	S&H	9 6 58	9B1	
Berwig Halt—Wrexham General (Croesnewydd North Jn)	GW	GW	1 1 31	20E5	
Bescot (Bescot South Jn)— **Darlaston**	LMS	LNW	5 5 41	13A2	
Bethesda—Bangor (Bethesda Junction)	LMR	LNW	3 12 51	19D2	52
Betley Road	LMS	LNW	1 10 45	20E2	
Bewdley—Shrewsbury (Sutton Bridge Junction)	LMR	GW	9 9 63	9/15B2	51
Bewdley—Woofferton:					
Bewdley—Tenbury Wells	WR	GW	1 8 62	9A1	57
Tenbury Wells—Woofferton	WR	S&H	31 7 61	9A1	*
Bieldside	LNE	GNS	5 4 37	37G4	
Bilbster	ScR	HR	13 6 60	38D2	
Billing	LMR	LNW	6 10 52	10B2	
Billinge Green Halt	LMS	LNW	2 3 42	20D2	
Bingham Road	ER	GN&LNW	2 7 51	16D3	
Birchfield Halt	ScR	GNS	7 5 56	36D1	
Birkenhead (Town)	BJ	BJ	7 5 45	45F4	
Birkenshaw & Tong	NER	GN	5 10 53	42B4	
Birmingham (New Street) (Grand Jn)—**Kings Norton**	LMS	Mid.	27 11 46	15G4	46
Birstall (Town)	NER	LNW	1 8 51	42B3	
Birtley	NER	NE	5 12 55	27C5	
Bishop Auckland—Stockton:					
Bishop Auckland (East Jn)— **Spennymoor**	LNE	NE	4 12 39	27D5	
Spennymoor—Stockton (Norton South Jn)	NER	NE	31 3 52	28E5	

ABOVE: *Ashover station on the Ashover Light Railway, photographed on October 23, 1926.*
[H. C. CASSERLEY

BELOW: *Class N 2-6-0 No. 31413 at Cirencester with the 1.52 p.m. Cheltenham—Southampton train on August 3, 1961.*
[L. A. DENCH

B

ABOVE: *G.W. 0-6-0PT No. 8732 arrives at Devynock and Sennybridge with the 11.25 a.m. Neath—Brecon train on September 29, 1962.* [W. G. SUMNER

BELOW: *Ivatt Class 2 2-6-0 No. 46524 emerges from the tunnel at Tal-y-Llyn Junction with the 10.25 a.m. from Brecon to Hereford on September 29, 1962.* [W. G. SUMNER

Station or line	Ownership at Closure	Pre-Group Company	Date Closed			Map Ref	Note
Bishop's Castle—Craven Arms (Stretford Bridge Jn)	BC	BC	20	4	35	14C1	*
Bishop's Cleeve Halt	WR	GW	7	3	60	9D4	
Bishops Stortford— Braintree & Bocking	ER	GE	3	3	52	11E4	
Bishops Waltham—Botley	SRy	LSW	2	1	33	4D3	14
Bishopstone Beach Halt	SRy	LBSC	1	1	42	5G4	58
Bisley—Brookwood	SR	LSW	21	7	52	5C1	*
Bittaford Platform	WR	GW	2	3	59	2D5	
Black Bank	ER	GE	17	6	63	17G4	
Blackburn (Daisyfield Junction) **—Hellifield**	LMR	LY	10	9	62	24E2	
Blackburn (Great Harwood Jn)**—Rose Grove** (via Padiham)	LMR	LY	2	12	57	24D1	
Blackford	ScR	Cal.	11	6	56	33F4	
Blackhall Rocks	NER	NE	4	1	60	28D4	
Blackhill—Birtley (Ouston Junction)	NER	NE	23	5	55	27C4	
Blackhill—Crook: Blackhill (Consett North Jn) **—Tow Law**	LNE	NE	1	5	39	27D4	1
Tow Law—Crook	NER	NE	11	6	56	27D5	
Black Lion Crossing Halt— Cwmaman	GW	GW	22	9	24	43D2	
Blackrod (Hindley & Blackrod Branch Jn)**—Hindley North** (Crow Nest Jn)	LMR	LY	4	1	60	45C2	
Blackwall—Stepney East	LNE	GE	4	5	26	40C2	23
Blackwood (Blackwood Jn)**— Tillietudlem** (Southfield Jn)	ScR	Cal.	1	10	51	30D5	66
Blaenau Ffestiniog (Central)—Bala	WR	GW	4	1	60	19F3	15
Blaenavon (Low Level)— Llantarnam	WR	GW	30	4	62	43A1	16
Blaengarw—Brynmenyn	WR	GW	9	2	53	43D3	
Blagdon—Congresbury	GW	GW	14	9	31	8D2	17
Blairadam	LNE	NB	22	9	30	30A3	
Blairgowrie—Coupar Angus	ScR	Cal.	10	1	55	33D5	
Blairhill & Gartsherrie (Sunnyside Jn)**—Bothwell**	ScR	NB	10	9	51	44C2	68
Blankney & Metheringham	ER	GN&GE	11	9	61	16B1	
Blantyre—Strathaven (Ctl)	LMS	Cal.	1	10	45	29C5	18
Blencow	LMR	CKP	3	3	52	26E1	19
Blenheim & Woodstock— Kidlington	WR	GW	1	3	54	10E4	*
Blisworth	LMR	LNW	4	1	60	10B3	
Blisworth—Northampton (Castle) (Duston Jn)	LMR	LNW	4	1	60	10B3	
Blisworth—Stratford-Upon- Avon (Old Town)	LMR/WR	SMJ	7	4	52	10B3	61
Blowick	LMS	LY	25	9	39	45F1	

Station or line	Ownership at Closure	Pre-Group Company	Date Closed			Map Ref	Note
Blunsdon	GW	MSW	28	9	24	9F5	
Blyton	ER	GC	2	2	59	22G5	
Boarhills	LNE	NB	22	9	30	34F3	
Boar's Head	LMR	LNW	31	1	49	45D2	
Boddam—Ellon	LNE	GNS	31	10	32	37D5	20
Bogside (Fife)	ScR	NB	15	9	58	30A4	
Bolton Abbey	LMS	Mid.	16	6	40	21C1	21
Bolton (Great Moor Street)— Kenyon Junction (Pennington South Jn)	LMR	LNW	29	3	54	45C2	50
Bolton (Great Moor Street)—Worsley (Fletcher St. Jn) (Roe Green Jn)	LMR	LNW	29	3	54	45C2	64
Bo'ness—Polmont (Bo'ness High Jn)	ScR	NB	7	5	56	30B4	
Bonnybridge—Greenhill	LMS	Cal.	28	7	30	30B5	
Bordon—Bentley	SR	LSW	16	9	57	4C1	
Borwick	LMR	FMJ	12	9	60	24B3	
Boston (Grand Sluice Jn)— **Woodhall Jn** (Coningsby Jn)	ER	GN	17	6	63	17C2	*
Botanic Gardens	LMS	Cal.	6	2	39	44E4	
Bothwell—Fallside (Bothwell Jn)	ScR	Cal.	5	6	50	44B2	*
Bottesford (East Jn)—**Harby & Stathern** (Stathern Jn)	ER	GN&LNW	7	12	53	16D2	
Bottesford (West Jn)—**Newark**	ER	GN	11	9	39	16C2	
Bott Lane Halt	LMR	LY	3	12	56	24D1✠	
Bourne (West Jn)—**Essendine**	ER	GN	18	6	51	17E1	*
Bourne (East Jn)—**Sleaford** (East Jn)	LNE	GN	22	9	30	17E1	47
Bournville—Lifford	LMS	Mid.	27	11	46	9A4	
Bower	ScR	HR	13	6	60	38C3	
Bowland	ScR	NB	7	12	53	30D1	
Bowling	ScR	Cal.	5	2	51	29B4	
Bowling Junction	NER	LY	3	12	51	42B4	
Bradbury	NER	NE	2	1	50	28E5	
Bradfield	ER	GE	2	7	56	12E4	
Bradley Fold (Bradley Fold Jn)—**Radcliffe (Central)**	LMR	LY	21	9	53	45B2	
Braidwood	ScR	Cal.	2	7	62	30D5	
Bramford	ER	GE	2	5	55	12D4	
Brampton Halt	LMS	NS	2	4	23	15C3✠	
Brampton (Town)— Brampton Junction	LNE	NE	29	10	23	27C1	26
Brandon & Wolston	LMR	LNW	12	9	60	10A5	
Branston & Heighington	ER	GN&GE	3	11	58	17B1	
Branston	LMS	Mid.	22	9	30	15E5	
Braunston & Willoughby	LMR	GC	1	4	57	10B4	
Brayton	MLR	M&C	5	6	50	26D2	
Breadsall	LMR	GN	6	4	53	41G2	
Brean Road Halt	WR	—	2	5	55	8E3✠	

Station or line	Ownership at Closure	Pre-Group Company	Date Closed	Map Ref	Note
Brecon—Neath (Riverside)					
(Neath N&B Jn)	WR	N&B	15 10 62	14F3	27
Brecon—Newport (Gaer Jn)	WR	BM	31 12 62	14F3	48
Breidden	WR	SWP	12 9 60	14A1✠	
Brentford—Southall	GW	GW	4 5 42	39D2	
Brentham Halt	GW	—	30 6 47	39C2✠	
Bridge of Dee	ScR	GSW	26 9 49	26C5	
Bridge of Dun—Forfar via					
Brechin	ScR	Cal.	4 8 52	34C3	28
Bridge of Earn—					
Ladybank	ScR	NB	19 9 55	34F5	
Bridgwater (North)—					
Edington Junction	WR	SD	1 12 52	8F3	29
Brigham—Bullgill Junction	LMS	M&C	29 4 35	26D3	*
Brill & Ludgershall Halt	WR	GW	7 1 63	10E3	
Brill—Quainton Road	LPTB	Met.	2 12 35	10E3	*
Brimington	ER	GC	2 1 56	41B2	56
Brindley Heath	LMR	—	6 4 59	15E4✠	
Brinklow	LMR	LNW	16 9 57	10A4	
Brinkworth	WR	GW	3 4 61	9G4	
Bristol (St. Philips)—					
Fishponds (Lawrence Hill Jn)	WR	Mid.	21 9 53	3G1	30
Bristol (Temple Meads)					
(North Somerset Jn)—**Frome**	WR	GW	2 11 59	3A2	
Briton Ferry—Cymmer Afan					
(East Jn)	WR	RSB	3 12 62	43F3	31
Briton Ferry (East)	GW	RSB	16 9 35	43F3	
Briton Ferry (West)	GW	GW	8 7 35	43F3	71
Brixham—Churston	WR	GW	13 5 63	2D3	*
Broadway	WR	GW	7 3 60	9C4	
Brock	LMS	LNW	1 5 39	24D3	
Brocketsbrae—Hamilton					
(Ferniegair Jn) via					
Tillietudlem	ScR	Cal.	1 10 51	30D5	67
Bromfield	WR	S&H	9 6 58	9A1	
Brooksby	LMR	Mid.	3 7 61	16E3	
Broomhouse	LNE	NB	24 9 27	44C3	
Broom Junction—					
Stratford-Upon-Avon	LMS	SMJ	16 6 47	9B4	65
Brotton—Marske (Saltburn					
West Jn)	NER	NE	15 1 51	28E3	32
Broughton Cross	LMS	LNW	2 3 42	26E3	
Broughton Gifford Halt	WR	GW	7 2 55	3B4	
Broughton Lane	ER	GC	3 4 56	42G2	
Broughton Lane (Tinsley					
South Jn)—**Stairfoot** (New					
Oaks Jn)	ER	GC	7 12 53	42G1	
Broughty Ferry—Forfar					
(North Jn)	ScR	Cal.	10 1 55	34E4	62
Browndown Halt	SRy	LSW	1 5 30	4E3	
Brownhills (Watling Street)					
—Aldridge	LMS	Mid.	31 3 30	15F4	33

Station or line	Ownership at Closure	Pre-Group Company	Date Closed			Map Ref	Note
Brymbo—Mold (Tryddyn Jn)	LMR/WR	LNW/ GW&LNW	27	3	50	20E4	34
Brynamman (East)— Swansea (St. Thomas)	WR	Mid.	25	9	50	43F1	
Brynamman (West)— Pantyffynon	WR	GW	18	8	58	43F1	35
Brynmawr—Newport (Bassaleg Jn)	WR	GW	30	4	62	43B2	36
Brynmawr—Pontypool (Trevethin Jn)	LMS	LNW	5	5	41	43A2	37
Bubwith	NER	NE	20	9	54	21D5	
Buckpool	ScR	GNS	7	3	60	37C1	
Bucksburn	ScR	GNS	5	3	56	37F4	
Bulford—Porton (Amesbury Jn)	SR	LSW	30	6	52	4C5	38
Bulkington	LMS	LNW	18	5	31	16G5	
Bullgill	LMR	M&C	7	3	60	26D3	
Bulwell Common	LMR	GC	4	3	63	41F4	
Bulwell Forest	LNE	GN	23	9	29	41F4	
Bulwell Hall Halt	LNE	GC	5	5	30	41F4✠	
Bunchrew	ScR	HR	13	6	60	36D5	
Bungalow Town Halt	SRy	LBSC	1	1	33	5F2	39
Burdett Road	LNE	GE	21	4	41	40C3	
Burlington Road Halt	LMS	PWY	11	9	39	24D4	
Burngullow	GW	GW	14	9	31	1D2	
Burnham-on-Sea— Highbridge (East)	WR	SD	29	10	51	8E3	40
Burnley (Manchester Road)	LMR	LY	6	11	61	24D1	
Burnmouth	ScR	NB	5	2	62	31C3	
Burrelton	ScR	Cal.	11	6	56	33E5	
Burry Port—Cwmmawr	WR	BPGV	21	9	53	7A2	
Burscough Bridge— Burscough Junction	LMR	LY	5	3	62	45E1	
Burton & Holme	LMR	LNW	27	3	50	24B3	
Burton Latimer	LMR	Mid.	20	11	50	10A2	25
Burton-on-Trent (North Stafford Jn)**—Tutbury** (Marston Jn)	LMR	NS	13	6	60	15D5	
Burton Point	LMR	GC	5	12	55	45F5	
Burton Salmon	NER	NE	14	9	59	42B1	
Bury St. Edmunds—Long Melford	ER	GE	14	4	61	12C5	41
Bury St. Edmunds—Thetford	ER	GE	8	6	53	12C5	42
Butterley—Langley Mill via Ripley	LMS	Mid.	1	6	30	41E2	43
Buttington	WR	Cam.	12	9	60	14A2	
Buxton—Rocester	LMR	LNW/NS	1	11	54	15B5	44
Buxworth	LMR	Mid.	15	9	58	15A4	45
Byfield (Woodford Jn)**— Woodford & Hinton**	ER	GC	31	5	48	10B4	
Byker	NER	NE	5	4	54	28A1	

1. Burnhill Jn—Tow Lawø.   2. Drymen—Gartness Jnø; Jamestown—Drymen *2.12.59.

3. *6.8.51. 4. Louth—Donington *15.9.56; Donington—Wragby* 1.12.58; Wragby—Bardney* 1.2.60. 5. Barnard Castle—Spring Gardens*. 6. Appleby (East)—Clifton Moor, Barnard Castle—Kirkby Stephen (Hartley Quarry)*. 7. Third side of triangle (East Loop—South Loop) opened for through running. 8. Barnton—Davidson's Mains*; Davidson's Mains—Craigleith* 1.6.60. 9. *6.7.53. 10. Temporary bus service since 4.4.60 withdrawn; Daybrook—Gedling Colliery*. 11. Picton—Stokesley* 1.12.58. 12. Harleston—Bungay* 1.2.60. 13. Beccles North Jn—Aldeby, Fleet Jn—St. Olaves*; St. Olaves—Yarmouth (South Town)* 1.2.60. 14. *30.4.62. 15. *28.1.61. Blaenau Festiniog (Ctl)—Trawsfyndd RO 18.11.63 and line connected to ex LNW branch. 16. Blaenavon (Low Level)—Pontypool (Trevethin Jn)*. 17. Blagdon—Wrington* 1.11.50; Wrington—Congresbury* 10.6.63. 18. High Blantyre—Strathaven (Ctl) *21.9.53; Blantyre—High Blantyre* 1.6.60. 19. RO 2.7.56. 20. *7.11.45. 21. RO 17.3.41. 22. RO 23.7.55. 23. The only portion remaining open is Limehouse—Millwall Jn, reached via NL line. 25. Formerly Isham. 26. *1.1.24. 27. Brecon—Sennybridge* 18.10.62; Sennybridge—Craig-y-nos*; Craig-y-nos—Colbren Jn* 7.10.63. 28. Brechin—Careston* 3.3.58. 29. *1.12.54 except Bridgwater North which was connected to and served from GW until 7.7.62. 30. Trains diverted to Temple Meads. 31. Workmen's trains continue to run between Cymmer Afan and Duffryn (Rhondda) Halt. Briton Ferry Jn—Burrows Jn (Port Talbot)*; Aberavon (Town)—Cwmavon *29.7.63. 32. *1.2.52. 33. Brownhills—Walsall Woodø. 34. Coed Talon—Bwlchgwyn Siding*. Bwlchgwyn Siding—Brymbo* 1.10.63. Coed Talon—Mold (Tryddyn Jn)* 22.7.63. 35. Brynamman (West)—Garnantø. 36. Brynmawr—Nantyglo was Brynmawr & Western Valleys Jt. (GW&LNW). Brynmawr—Coalbrookvale Sdgs (1m. south of Nantyglo)* 4.11.63.. 37. Brynmawr—Blaenavon (High Level)* 24.6.54. Trevethin Jn—Abersychan & Talywain was GW. 38. Newton Tony—Amesbury Jn*. Freight trains ran via Grateley until 4.3.63. Bulford Camp—Newton Tony* 4.3.63. 39. RO 1.7.35 as Shoreham Airport (Bungalow Town) Halt. qv. 40. *20.5.63. 41. Lavenham—Long Melford*. 42. *27.6.60. 43. Butterley—Ripley, Marehay Jn—Heanorø; Heanor—Bailey Brook Collieryø. 44. Ashbourne—Hartington* 7.10.63. Ashbourne—Rocester* 1.6.64. 45. Formerly Bugsworth. 46. PC. TC 27.1.41. 47. Billingborough—Sleaford (East Jn)* 28.7.56; Bourne—Billingborough* 15.6.64. 48. Fleur-de-Lis Platform—Bedwas*; Deri Jn—Pant* 11.8.63, Pant—Brecon* 4.5.64. 49. Buchlyvie—Port of Menteithø; Port of Menteith—Stirling* 5.10.59. 50. Atherton Jn—Pennington South Jn* 17.6.63. 51. Highley (Alveley Colliery)—Shrewsbury* 2.12.63. 52. *7.10.63. 53. *2.12.63, but Banbury (Merton St) Yard served from GW line. 54. Bacup—Facit*; Facit—Whitworth* 11.8.63. 55. *19.6.33. 56. Formerly Sheepbridge. 57. Tenbury Wells—Cleobury Mortimer* 6.1.64. 58. Formerly Bishopstone, RN 26.9.38 when new Bishopstone station opened near Seaford. 59. Shefford—Hitchin* 30.12.63. 60. Bedford (Oakley Jn)—Piddington* 6.1.64. 61. Blisworth (Ironstone Siding)—Byfield (Woodford West Jn)* 3.2.64. 62. Forfar North Jn—Kingsmuir* 8.12.58. 63. Barnsley (West Jn)—Barnsley Main Colliery, Cudworth (West Jn)—Cudworth (South Jn)*. 64. Little Hulton—Worsley (Roe Green Jn)* -.1.61. 65. *-.5.60. 66. *4.1.60. 67. Brocketsbrae—Southfield Jnø; Southfield Jn—Dalserf* 4.1.60; Dalserf—Ferniegair Jn* 20.4.64. 68. Whifflet North Jn—Bothwellø. 69. Fauldhouse—Jn with Kingshill Colliery Branchø. 70. *5.10.59. 71. Replaced by new station, Briton Ferry.

Station or line	Ownership at Closure	Pre-Group Company	Date Closed			Map Ref	Note
Cadoxton—Treforest							
(Treforest Jn)	WR	BRY	10	9	62	43C4	23
Caerleon	WR	GW	30	4	62	43A3	
Cairntable Halt	ScR	—	3	4	50	29F4✠	
Caldy	LMR	BJ	1	2	54	20C5	
Calthwaite	LMR	LNW	7	4	52	27D1	
Calveley	LMR	LNW	7	3	60	15B1	
Calvert	LMR	GC	4	3	63	10D3	

Station or line	Ownership at Closure	Pre-Group Company	Date Closed			Map Ref	Note
Camels Head Halt	SRy	LSW	4	5	42	1D5✠	
Camerton	LMR	LNW	3	3	52	26E3	
Camerton (Marron West Jn)—							
Moor Row	LMS	WCE	13	4	31	26E3	2
Canada Dock—Spellow							
(Atlantic Dock Jn)	LMS	LNW	5	5	41	45F3	3
Canterbury West—							
Shorncliffe:							
Canterbury West							
(Harbledown Jn)—**Lyminge**	SRy	SEC	2	12	40	6C3	4
Lyminge—Shorncliffe							
(Cheriton Jn)	SRy	SEC	16	6	47	6D3	*5
Cardiff Parade	GW	Rhy	15	4	28	43B4	
Cardigan—Whitland							
(Cardigan Jn)	WR	GW	10	9	62	13E2	6
Cargill	ScR	Cal.	11	6	56	33E5	
Carham	ScR	NE	4	7	55	31D2	
Carlton-on-Trent	ER	GN	2	3	53	16B2	
Carmarthen (Abergwili Jn)—							
Llandilo	WR	LNW	9	9	63	13G3	*
Carmarthen Junction	GW	GW	27	9	26	13G4	
Carmont	ScR	Cal.	11	6	56	34B2	
Carmyllie—Elliott Jn	D&A	D&A	2	12	29	34D3	
Carn Brea	WR	GW	2	1	61	1E5	
Carrington	LNE	GC	24	9	28	41F4	
Carronbridge	ScR	GSW	7	12	53	30G4	
Cassillis	ScR	GSW	6	12	54	29F3	
Castle Eden—Murton	NER	NE	9	6	52	28D5	
Castleford (Central)—							
Garforth	NER	NE	22	1	51	42B1	
Castle Howard	LNE	NE	22	9	30	22B5	
Castor	ER	LNW	1	7	57	11A1	
Caton	LMR	Mid.	1	5	61	24B3	
Catrine—Mauchline							
(Brackenhill Jn)	LMS	GSW	3	5	43	29E5	
Cauldcots	LNE	NB	22	9	30	34D3	
Causewayhead	ScR	NB	4	7	55	30A5	
Cawood—Selby (Wistow Jn)	LNE	NE	1	1	30	21D5	7
Caythorpe	ER	GN	10	9	62	16C1	
Cayton	NER	NE	5	5	52	22A3	
Cefn	WR	GW	12	9	60	20F4	
Chacewater (Blackwater East							
Jn)—**Newquay** (Tolcarn Jn)	WR	GW	4	2	63	1D1	8
Chalcombe Road Halt	LMR	GC	6	2	56	10C4	
Chalvey Halt	GW	GW	7	7	30	5B1✠	
Chappel & Wakes Colne—							
Haverhill	ER	CVH	1	1	62	12E5	9
Chard Junction—Taunton:							
Chard (Junction)—Chard							
(Central)	WR	LSW	10	9	62	3E1	
Chard (Central)—Taunton							
(Creech Jn)	WR	GW	10	9	62	3E1	1

Station or line	Ownership at Closure	Pre-Group Company	Date Closed	Map Ref	Note
Charlestown—Dunfermline (Elbowend Jn)	LNE	NB	1 11 26	30B3	
Charlton Halt	LMS	LNW	25 10 26	10E4	
Charlton Mackrell	WR	GW	10 9 62	3D2	
Charlton Marshall Halt	SR	—	17 9 56	3E4✠	
Charwelton	LMR	GC	4 3 63	10B4	
Chatterley	LMR	NS	27 9 58	15C3	
Cheadle—Cresswell	LMR	NS	17 6 63	15C4	
Checker House	LNE	GC	14 9 31	16A3	
Chellaston (East Jn)—**Trent** (Sheet Stores Jn)	LMS	Mid.	22 9 30	16D4	
Cheltenham Spa (Malvern Road) (Lansdown Jn)— **Kingham**	WR	GW	15 10 62	9D4	10
Chequerbent	LMR	LNW	3 3 52	45C2	
Cheriton Halt	SRy	SEC	16 6 47	6D2✠	11
Cherry Burton	NER	NE	5 1 59	22D4	
Cherry Tree (Jn)—**Chorley**	LMR	LUJ	4 1 60	24E2	
Cheshunt—Lower Edmonton (Bury St. Jn)	GE	GE	2 7 19	11G3	12
Chester (General) (Mold Jn)—**Ruthin**	LMR	LNW	30 4 62	20D4	13
Chester (General) (Tattenhall Jn)—**Whitchurch**	LMR	LNW	16 9 57	20D4	14
Chesterfield (Market Place) —Lincoln (Central): **Chesterfield (Market Place) —Shirebrook (North)**	ER	GC	3 12 51	41C2	15
Shirebrook (North)—Lincoln (Central) (Pyewipe Jn)	ER	GC	19 9 55	16B4	37
Chesterfield (Mid) (Tapton Jn)—**Elmton & Cresswell**	ER	Mid.	5 7 54	41B2	
Chester (Liverpool Road)	LMR	GC	3 12 51	20D4	
Chettisham	ER	GE	13 6 60	11B4	
Chevington	NER	NE	15 9 58	31G5	
Chichester (Fishbourne Crossing)—**Midhurst**	SRy	LBSC	8 7 35	4E1	16
Childwall	CLC	CLC	1 1 31	45E4	
Chiltern Green	LMR	Mid.	7 4 52	11F1	
Chipping Sodbury	WR	GW	3 4 61	8C1	
Chorley (Adlington Jn)— **Wigan (NW)** (Boar's Head Jn)	LMR	LUJ	4 1 60	45D1	
Christchurch—Ringwood	SRy	LSW	30 9 35	4F5	*
Christon Bank	NER	NE	15 9 58	31E5	
Church Brampton	LMS	LNW	18 5 31	10B3	
Church Road	LMS	Mid.	1 1 25	15G4	
Church Road Halt	WR	BM	16 9 57	43B3	
Churwell	LMS	LNW	2 12 40	42B3	
Cinderford—Speech House Road (Serridge Jn)	SVW	SVW	8 7 29	9E2	17
Cinderford—Newnham (Bullo Pill West)	WR	GW	3 11 58	9E2	18

Station or line	Ownership at Closure	Pre-Group Company	Date Closed			Map Ref	Note
Clapham (Yorks)—**Low Gill**	LMR	LNW/Mid.	1	2	54	24B1	
Claxby & Usselby	ER	GC	7	3	60	22G3	
Claydon	LMR	GC	4	3	63	12D4	
Claypole	ER	GN	16	9	57	16C2	
Cleckheaton (Spen)	NER	LNW	5	10	53	42B4	
Cledford Bridge Halt	LMS	LNW	2	3	42	20D2	
Cleeve	LMR	Mid.	20	2	50	9D3	
Cliburn	LMR	NE	17	9	56	27E1	
Cliff Common	NER	NE	20	9	54	21D5	
Cliff Common—York (Layerthorpe)	DVL	DVL	1	9	26	21D5	
Clifton & Lowther	LMS	LNW	4	7	38	27E1	
Clifton Mill	LMR	LNW	6	4	53	10A4	
Clifton Road (Brighouse)	LMS	LY	14	9	31	42C4	
Clocksbriggs	ScR	Cal.	5	12	55	34D4	
Closeburn	ScR	GSW	11	9	61	26A4	
Clowne South	LNE	GC	10	9	39	41B4	
Clunes	ScR	HR	13	6	60	35D5	
Clydebank (East)—**Yoker** (Clydebank Jn)	ScR	NB	14	9	59	44F4	*
Clynderwen—Fishguard & Goodwick (Letterston Jn) via Rosebush	GW	GW	25	10	37	13F2	19
Clyst St. Mary & Digby Halt	SR	LSW	27	9	48	2B3✠	
Coalpit Heath	WR	GW	3	4	61	8C1	
Coalport (East)—**Hadley**	WR	LNW	2	6	52	15F2	20
Coalville (East)	LMS	LNW	13	4	31	16E4	
Coatbridge (Sunnyside) (Greenside Jn)—**Manuel**	LNE	NB	1	5	30	30C5	
Coborn Road	LNE	GE	8	12	46	40C3	
Cockburnspath	ScR	NB	18	6	51	31B2	
Cockfield Fell	NER	NE	15	9	58	27E4	
Codford	SR	GW	19	9	55	3C5	
Colbren Jn—Pontardawe (Ynysygeinon Jn)	GW	N&B	12	9	32	43E1	21
Colefords—Parkend (Coleford Branch Jn)	SVW	SVW	8	7	29	9E1	
Collins Green	LMR	LNW	2	4	51	45D3	
Colwich	LMR	LNW & NS	3	2	58	15E4	
Condover Halt	WR	S&H	9	6	58	14B1	
Congleton (Upper Jn)—**Bucknall & Northwood** (Milton Jn)	LMS	NS	11	7	27	15B3	39
Coniston—Foxfield	LMR	Fur.	6	10	58	26G2	22
Conon	ScR	HR	13	6	60	35D5	
Coombes Holloway Halt	GW	GW	5	12	27	15G4✠	
Cooper Bridge	LMR	LY	20	2	50	42C4	
Cooper Bridge (Anchor Pit Jn)—**Wyke & Norwood Green**	LMS	LY	14	9	31	42C4	
Copley	LMS	LY	20	7	31	42C5	
Copmanthorpe	NER	NE	5	1	59	21C5	
Corby Glen	ER	GN	15	6	59	16D1	

ABOVE: *A train of the Bishops Castle Railway photographed in May 1932.* [H. C. CASSERLEY

BELOW: *Metropolitan 4-4-0T No. 23 approaches Wood siding on the Quainton Road—Brill branch on June 22, 1935, the year in which the service was withdrawn. This locomotive has since been preserved and is now in Clapham Museum.* [H. C. CASSERLEY

ABOVE: *G.W. 2-6-2T No. 4100 takes water at Chipping Norton with the 4.25 p.m. train to Kingham on September 15, 1962.*
[W. G. SUMNER

BELOW: *Ivatt Class 2 2-6-2T No. 41217 stands under the overall roof at Coniston with the 7.22 a.m. train to Foxfield on July 26, 1958.*
[G. DANIELS

Station or line	Ownership at Closure	Pre-Group Company	Date Closed	Map Ref	Note
Corfe Mullen Halt	SR	—	17 9 56	3F5✠	
Cornholme	LMS	LY	26 9 38	21E1	
Cornwood	WR	GW	2 3 59	2D5	
Corringham—Coryton	CL	CL	3 3 52	6A5✠	
Corwen—Rhyl:					
Corwen—Ruthin	LMR	LNW	3 2 52	19F5	22
Ruthin—Denbigh	LMR	LNW	30 4 62	19E5	38
Denbigh (Mold & Denbigh Jn)—**Rhyl** (Foryd Jn)	LMR	LNW	19 9 55	19D5	
Cotehill	LMR	Mid.	7 4 52	27C1	
Coughton	WR	Mid.	30 6 52	9B4	
County School—Wroxham	ER	GE	15 9 52	18E4	24
Court Sart	GW	RSB	16 9 35	43F3	
Court Sart (Neath Jn RSB)—**Neath (Canal Side)**	GW	RSB	16 9 35	43F3	
Cove Bay	ScR	Cal.	11 6 56	34A1	
Cowbit	ER	GN&GE	11 9 61	17E2	
Cowton	NER	NE	15 9 58	28F5	
Craigo	ScR	Cal.	11 6 56	34C3	
Cranford	LMR	Mid.	2 4 56	10A1	
Craven Arms—Wellington:					
Craven Arms (Marsh Farm Jn)—**Much Wenlock**	WR	GW	31 12 51	14C1	25
Much Wenlock—Wellington (Ketley Jn)	WR	GW	23 7 62	15F2	26
Creigiau (Tyn-y-caeau Jn)—**St. Fagans**	WR	BRY	10 9 62	43D4	27
Criggion—Kinnerley Jn:					
Criggion—Melverley	S&M	S&M	– 10 32	14A2	28
Melverley—Kinnerley Jn	S&M	S&M	6 11 33	14A2	28
Crofton	LMS	LY	30 11 31	42C1	
Cromer (Beach) (Roughton Road Jn)—**Mundesley-on-Sea**	ER	NSJ	7 4 53	18D3	*
Cromer (High)—Gunton (Cromer Jn)	ER	GE	20 9 54	18D3	29
Cromer **(Newstead Lane Jn—Runton West Jn)**	ER	NSJ	20 9 54	18D3	30
Cropredy	WR	GW	17 9 56	10C4	
Crosby Garrett	LMR	Mid.	6 10 52	27F2	
Crossgates	ScR	NB	26 9 49	30A3	
Crossgates (Cowdenbeath South Jn)—**Lochgelly** (Lumphinnans Ctl Jn) via Cowdenbeath Old	NB	NB	31 3 19	30A3	
Crossgatehall Halt	LNE	NB	22 9 30	30B ✠	31
Cross Lane	LMR	LNW	20 7 59	45B3	
Crowden	LMR	GC	4 2 57	21F2	
Crown St. Halt	LMR	—	7 6 49	15C3✠	
Crow Park	ER	GN	6 10 58	16B2	
Croxall	LMS	Mid.	9 7 28	15E5	
Croxdale	LNE	NE	26 9 38	27D5	

Station or line	Ownership at Closure	Pre-Group Company	Date Closed	Map Ref	Note
Crystal Palace (HL)—					
Nunhead	SR	SEC	20 9 54	40F4	*32
Cudworth—Hull:					
Cudworth—South Howden	LNE	HB	1 1 32	21F3	36
South Howden—Hull					
(Walton St. Jn)	NER	HB	1 8 55	22E5	33
Culkerton	WR	GW	5 3 56	9F3	34
Culworth	LMR	GC	29 9 58	10C4	
Cummersdale	LMR	M&C	18 6 51	26C1	
Cummertrees	ScR	GSW	19 9 55	26B3	
Cumwhinton	LMR	Mid.	5 11 56	26C1	
Cunninghamhead	ScR	GSW	1 1 51	29D3	
Curthwaite	LMR	M&C	12 6 50	26C1	
Currie Hill	ScR	Cal.	2 4 51	30C3	
Cynonville Halt	WR	RSB	2 1 56	43E3	
Cymmer Afan—Near					
Blaengwynfi	WR	RSB	13 6 60	43E2	35
Cymmer (General)	WR	RSB	13 6 60	43E2	

1. *6.7.64. **2.** Marron W. Jn—Ullock Jn* 3.5.54. **3.** See also Alexandra Dock. **4.** *16.6. 47 **5.** Cl. 3.5.43, RO 7.10.46. **6.** *27.5.63. **7.** *2.5.60. **8.** Blackwater E. Jn—Trevemper Sdg (1m 20ch from Newquay)*; Trevemper Sdg—Tolcarn Jn* 7.12.63. **9.** Yeldham—Haverhill*. **10.** Lansdown Jn—Bourton-on-the-Water*. **11.** Cl. 1.12.15, RO 14.6.20, Cl. 1.2.41, RO 7.10.46. **12.** Cl. 1.10.09, RO 1.3.15; RO on electrification 21.11.60 and Churchbury RN Southbury, Forty Hill RN Turkey St. **13.** Denbigh—Rhydymwyn*; workmen's service withdrawn from Chester—Broughton 2.9.63. **14.** *4.11.63 but Sunday diversions travelled this way until 8.12.63. **15.** Chesterfield—Arkwright (Town)* 4.3.57; Arkwright (Town)— Shirebrook (North)*. **16.** Cocking—Midhurst* 20.11.51 (landslide); Lavant—Cocking* 31.8.53. **17.** Cinderford served by GW trains until 3.11.63. **18.** Cinderford station was SVW & GW Jt. **19.** Clynderwen—Letterston* 16.5.49. **20.** Coalport—Dawley & Stirchley* 5.12.60. **21.** Abercrave—Ynysygeinon Jn* 17.6.63. **22.** *30.4.62. **23.** *17.6.63. **24.** Foulsham—Reepham*; Themelthorpe (MGN crossing)—Reepham RO to freight 12.9.60. **25.** Marsh Farm Jn—Longville*; Longville—Much Wenlock (officially)* 2.12.63 but lifting commenced on 28.10.63. **26.** Much Wenlock—Buildwas* 19.1.64; Ketley— Ketley Jn* 23.7.62. Buildwas remained open until 9.9.63 on Bewdley—Shrewsbury line. **27.** *17.6.63. **28.** *4.1.60. **29.** *7.3.60. **30.** *12.9.60. **31.** Cl. 1.1.17, RO 1.2.19. **32.** Cl. 1.1.17, RO 1.3.19, Cl. 22.5.44, RO 4.3.46. **33.** South Howden—Little Weighton* 6.4.58; Little Weighton—Hull (Springbank Jn)* 6.7.64. **34.** RO as halt 2.2.59. **35.** Realignment of RSB line on formation of closed Abergwynfi branch. **36.** Wrangbrook Jn—South Howden *6.4.58. **37.** Edwinstowe remained open until 2.1.56. **38.** See also Chester—Ruthin entry on Page 23. **39.** Trains reversed at Congleton (Upper Jn.).

Station or line	Ownership at Closure	Pre-Group Company	Date Closed	Map Ref	Note
Dairsie	ScR	NB	20 9 54	34F4	
Daisyfield	LMR	LY	3 11 58	24D2	
Dalkeith—Millerhill					
(Glenesk Jn)	LNE	NB	5 1 42	30C2	
Dalmeny (South Jn)—Gogar					
(Kirkliston Jn)	LNE	NB	22 9 30	30B3	

Station or line	Ownership at Closure	Pre-Group Company	Date Closed	Map Ref	Note
Dalrymple	ScR	GSW	6 12 54	29F3	
Dalserf—Stonehouse (East Jn)	LMS	Cal.	7 1 35	30D5	21
Damems	LMR	Mid.	23 5 49	21D1	
Danby Wiske	NER	NE	15 9 58	28G5	
Dandaleith	ScR	GNS	5 3 62	36D1	
Darcy Lever	LMR	LY	29 10 51	45B2	
Daresbury	LMR	BJ	7 7 52	45D4	
Darfield	ER	Mid.	17 6 63	42E1	
Darras Hall—South Gosforth	LNE	NE	17 6 29	27B5	1
Darvel—Strathaven	LMS	GSW/Cal.	25 9 39	29E5	2
Dauntsey—Somerford (Kingsmead Crossing)	GW	GW	16 7 33	9G4	*24
Daybrook—Nottingham (London Road) (HL) (Trent Lane West Jn)	LNE	GN	14 9 31	41F5	3
Daybrook (Leen Valley Jn)— **Shirebrook North**	LNE	GN	14 9 31	41F5	4
Dearham Bridge	LMR	M&C	5 6 50	26D3	
Deepcar	ER	GC	15 6 59	42F3	
Denaby Halt	ER	DV	1 1 49	21F4	
Delny	ScR	HR	13 6 60	36C5	
Delph—Greenfield (Delph Jn)	LMR	LNW	2 5 55	21F1	5
Denny (Denny West Jn)— **Greenhill** (Carmuirs West Jn)	LMS	Cal.	28 7 30	30B5	
Denny—Larbert (Bonnywater Jn)	LMS	Cal.	28 7 30	30B5	
Denton Halt	SR	SEC	4 12 61	5B5✠	
Denton **(Ashton Moss Jn— Crowthorn Jn)**	LMR	LNW	4 5 59	45A3	
Denton (Denton Jn)— **Stalybridge**	LMR	LNW	25 9 50	21A2	
Derwydd Road	WR	GW	3 5 54	43G1	
Dewsbury (Market Place)— Horbury & Ossett (Thornhill Midland Jn)	LMS	LY	1 12 30	42C3	
Dewsbury **(Headfield Jn— West Jn)**	LMS	LY	1 12 30	42C3	*
Dicconson Lane & Aspull	LMR	LY	1 2 54	45C2	
Didcot—Newbury	WR	GW	10 9 62	10F4	23
Digby	ER	GN&GE	11 9 61	17C1	
Dinas Jn	LMR	LNW	10 9 51	19E2	
Dinas Mawddwy—Cemmes Road	GW	Cam.	1 1 31	14A4	6
Dingle—Seaforth & Litherland	LOR	LOR	31 12 56	45F3✠	*
Dinmore	WR	S&H	9 6 58	9B1	
Dinwoodie	ScR	Cal.	13 6 60	26A3	
Dirleton	ScR	NB	1 2 54	31B1	
Distington—Oatlands	CWJ	CWJ	– 9 22	26E3	7

Station or line	Ownership at Closure	Pre-Group Company	Date Closed			Map Ref	Note
Distington—Rowrah	LMS	WCE	1	1	27	26E3	
Ditchford	LMS	LNW	1	11	24	10A1	
Ditton Jn—Timperley	LMR	LNW	10	9	62	45E4	22
Ditton Priors—Cleobury Mortimer	GW	CMDP	26	9	38	15G1	8
Dixon Fold	LMS	LY	18	5	31	45B2	
Dodworth	ER	GC	29	6	59	42E3	
Doe Hill	LMR	Mid.	12	9	60	41D3	
Dolphinton—Carstairs (Dolphinton Jn)	LMS	Cal.	4	6	45	30D3	9
Dolphinton—Leadburn	LNE	NB	1	4	33	30D3	*
Doncaster (Shaftholme Jn)— **Knottingley**	LMS	LY	10	3	47	21F5	
Doncaster (Potteric Carr Jn)— **Shireoaks** (Brancliffe Jn)	SYJ	SYJ	2	12	29	21G2	20
Donibristle Halt	ScR	—	2	11	59	30B3✠	
Donington Road	ER	GN&GE	11	9	61	17D2	
Don Street	LNE	GNS	5	4	37	37F4	
Dornoch—The Mound	ScR	HR	13	6	60	36B4	*
Dorrington	WR	S&H	9	6	58	14B1	
Dorton Halt	WR	—	7	1	63	10E3✠	
Dovecliffe	ER	GC	7	12	53	42E2	
Dover (Harbour)	SRy	SEC	10	7	27	6D2	
Dowlais (Central)—**Pant**	WR	BM	2	5	60	43C2	10
Drayton	SRy	LBSC	1	6	30	5F1	
Driffield—Malton	NER	NE	5	6	50	22C4	12
Drighlington	NER	GN	1	1	62	42B4	
Drum	ScR	GNS	10	9	51	34A2	
Drumburgh	LMR	NB	4	7	55	26C2	
Drumlithie	ScR	Cal.	11	6	56	34B2	
Drumshoreland	ScR	NB	18	6	51	30B3	
Drybrook—Bilson Jn	GW	GW	7	7	30	8A1	11
Dubton Junction	ScR	Cal.	4	8	52	34C3	
Dudley Hill	NER	GN	7	4	52	42B4	
Dukeries Junction	ER	GC	6	3	50	16B2	
Dukeries Junction	ER	GN	6	3	50	16B2	
Dukinfield & Ashton	LMR	LNW	25	9	50	21A2	
Dukinfield (Central)	LMR	GC	4	5	59	21A2	
Dulverton (Morebath Jn)— **Exeter St. Davids** (Stoke Canon Jn)	WR	GW	7	10	63	7F5	19
Dumbarton (East Jn)— **Bowling** (Jn with new connection)	ScR	NB	25	4	60	29B4	*
Dumfries House	ScR	GSW	13	6	49	29F4	
Dumfries—Lockerbie	ScR	Cal.	19	5	52	26B3	
Dundee (East)	ScR	D&A	5	1	59	34E4	13
Dundee (Esplanade)	LNE	NB	2	10	39	34E4	14
Dungeness—Lydd (Lydd Jn)	SRy	SEC	4	7	37	6E3	15
Dunham Hill	LMR	BJ	7	4	52	20D3	
Dunning	ScR	Cal.	11	6	56	33F4	

Station or line	Ownership at Closure	Pre-Group Company	Date Closed	Map Ref	Note
Dunstable (North)— **Leighton Buzzard**	LMR	LNW	2 7 62	10D1	
Dunston-on-Tyne— Newcastle (King Edward Bridge West Jn)	LNE	NE	4 5 26	28B2	
Durham—Scotswood: **Durham** (Relly Mill Jn)— **Blackhill** (Consett North Jn)	LNE	NE	1 5 39	27D5	
Blackhill—Scotswood (Scotswood Bridge Jn)	NER	NE	1 2 54	27C4	16
Durham (Elvet)— **Sunderland:** **Durham (Elvet)—** **Pittington**	LNE	NE	1 1 31	28D5	17
Pittington—Sunderland (Ryhope Grange Jn)	NER	NE	5 1 53	28D5	18
Dursley—Coaley	WR	Mid.	10 9 62	9F2	
Dyke, The—see The Dyke					
Dyserth—Prestatyn	LMS	LNW	22 9 30	19C5	

1. Darras Hall—Ponteland* 2.8.54. **2.** Actually closed 11.9.39. **3.** *31.7.51. Intermediate stations closed 13.7.16. **4.** Kirkby-in-Ashfield (S. Jn)—Sutton-in-Ashfield (Town) RO 20.2.56, Cl. 17.9.56; Service ran to Nottingham (Vic) via Hucknall (GC). **5.** *4.11.63. **6.** Cl. 17.4.01 as Mawddwy Ry; RO 31.7.11 by Cambrian Ry; *1.7.51. **7.** Cl. –.7.92, RO –.11.09, Cl. 1.1.17, RO –.7.17. **8.** Transferred to Admiralty 1.1.57. **9.** Cl. 12.9.32, RO 17.7.33, **10.** Trains actually ran until 6.5.60. *4.5.64. **11.** Drybrook—Whimsey* –.–.58. **12.** *20.10.58. **13.** Trains diverted to Dundee (Tay Bridge). **14.** Formerly Tay Bridge. **15.** See also New Romney. **16.** Lintz Green—Blaydon* 11.11.63. **17.** *11.1.54. **18.** Pittington—Murton*. **19.** Morebath Jn—Thorverton (excl. Tiverton)*. **20.** Dinnington Jn—Brancliffe Jn was GC & Mid. Jt. **21.** Dalserf Jn—Swinehill* 20.4.64; Swinehill— Stonehouse (East Jn)ø. **22.** Broadheath Jn—Timperley*. **23.** Cl. (P) 4.8.42, RO 18.4.43. **24.** From this date, service diverted to Little Somerford via a new connection from Kingsmead Crossing.

Station or line	Ownership at Closure	Pre-Group Company	Date Closed	Map Ref	Note
Eardisley—Titley	GW	GW	1 7 40	14E1	*
Earl's Court—Willesden Junction	WL/LMS	WL/LNW	20 10 40	39D5	1
Earlsheaton	NER	GN	8 6 53	42C3	
Easingwold—Alne	Eas.	Eas.	29 11 48	21B4	12
Eassie	ScR	Cal.	11 6 56	34D5	
East Grange	ScR	NB	15 9 58	30A4	
East Grinstead—Lewes (Culver Junction)	SR	LBSC	17 3 58	5D4	*2
East Ham (Little Ilford No. 1)— **Woodgrange Park** (East Ham Loop North Jn)	ER	Mid.	15 9 58	40B2	*
Easton—Melcombe Regis	SR	ECH	3 3 52	3G3	3

Station or line	Ownership at Closure	Pre-Group Company	Date Closed			Map Ref	Note
East Ville	ER	GN	11	9	61	17C3	
Eastwood	LMR	LY	3	12	51	21E1	
Ebbsfleet & Cliffsend Halt	SRy	SEC	1	4	33	6B1✠	
Ebbw Vale (Low Level)— Aberbeeg	WR	GW	30	4	62	43B1	
Ebbw Vale (High Level)— Beaufort (Ebbw Vale Jn)	WR	LNW	5	2	51	43B1	4
Ebchester	NER	NE	21	9	53	27C4	
Ecclefechan	ScR	Cal.	13	6	60	26B2	
Edderton	ScR	HR	13	6	60	36B5	
Edenbridge (**Crowhurst Jn North—Crowhurst Jn South**)	SR	CO	13	6	55	5D4	
Edgware—Highgate: **Edgware—Finchley** (Church End)	LNE	GN	11	9	39	5A2	13
East Finchley—Highgate	LNE	GN	3	3	41	39A5	14
Edinburgh (Haymarket Central Jn)—**Portobello** (Niddrie North) via Duddingston	ScR	NB	10	9	62	30F2	5
Edington & Bratton	WR	GW	3	11	52	3B4	
Edlington—Wakefield (Kirkby Jn) (Crofton W. Jn)	NER/ER	LY/DV	10	9	51	21G2	
Edwalton	LMS	Mid.	28	7	41	41G5	
Edwinstowe— **Hollinwell & Annesley** (Kirkby South Jn)	LMR/ER	GC	2	1	56	41C5	
Edzell—Brechin	LMS	Cal.	27	9	38	34C3	6
Efail Isaf (Tonteg Jn)— **Trehafod**	GW	BRY	10	7	30	43C4	ø
Egginton Junction	LMR	NS&GN	5	3	62	16D5	
Egginton Junction—Derby (Friargate)	LNE	GN	4	12	39	16D5	
Elford	LMR	Mid.	31	3	52	15E5	
Elland	NER	LY	10	9	62	42C5	
Ellenbrook	LMR	LNW	2	1	61	45B2	
Ellesmere—Wrexham (Ctl)	WR	Cam.	10	9	62	20F4	7
Elmore Halt	SRy	LSW	1	5	30	4E3	
Elslack	LMR	Mid.	3	3	52	21C1	
Elton	ER	LNW	7	12	53	11A1	
Ely (Sutton Branch Jn)—**St. Ives** (Needingworth Jn)	LNE	GE	2	2	31	11B4	8
Embleton	LMR	CKP	15	9	58	26E2	
Enthorpe	NER	NE	20	9	54	22C4	
Epsom (Town)	SRy	LBSC	3	3	29	5C2	
Escrick	NER	NE	8	6	53	21D5	
Esholt	LMS	Mid.	28	10	40	21D2	
Eskbank & Dalkeith— Galashiels: **Eskbank & Dalkeith** (Hardengreen Jn)—**Rosewell & Hawthornden**	ScR	NB	10	9	62	30C2	

Station or line	Ownership at Closure	Pre-Group Company	Date Closed	Map Ref	Note
Rosewell & Hawthornden— Galashiels (Kilnknowe Jn)	ScR	NB	5 2 62	30E1	*
Eskbridge	LNE	NB	22 9 30	30C2	
Eskmeals	LMR	Fur.	3 8 59	26G3	
Essendine	ER	GN	15 6 59	16E1	
Essendine—Stamford (Town)	ER	GN/Mid.	15 6 59	16E1	*
Esslemont	ScR	GNS	15 9 52	37E4	
Eston—Cargo Fleet	LNE	NE	11 3 29	28E4	
Evanton	ScR	HR	13 6 60	36C5✠	
Evenwood	NER	NE	14 10 57	27E5	
Everingham	NER	NE	20 9 54	22D5	
Exeter (St. Thomas) (City Basin Jn)—**Heathfield**	WR	GW	9 6 58	2B3	10
Eydon Road Platform	LMR	GC	2 4 56	10C4	
Eye Green	ER	MGN	2 12 57	17F2	
Eye—Mellis	LNE	GE	2 2 31	12B4	
Eyemouth—Burnmouth	ScR	NB	5 2 62	31C3	*11

1. Bomb damage. **2.** Originally closed 13.6.55 (actually 28.5.55 due to ASLEF strike). Horsted Keynes—Culver Jn*. RO 7.8.56 with the statutory minimum of 4 trains daily. Horsted Keynes—Sheffield Park leased to Bluebell Rly. Co. and RO 7.8.60 to Bluebell Halt ($\frac{1}{4}$ mile south of Horsted Keynes). Service extended to Horsted Keynes (BR) on 29.10.61. **3.** Portland—Melcombe Regis was SR (WP). **4.** *2.11.59. **5.** Niddrie North—Craiglockart Jn still used on Sundays. **6.** Cl. 27.4.38, RO 4.7.38. **7.** Cl. 10.6.40 RO 6.5.46. Ellesmere—Bangor-on-Dee.* **8.** Sutton—Bluntisham* 6.10.58. **10.** City Basin Jn—Christow*; Christow—Trusham* 1.5.61. **11.** Cl. 13.8.48 (Floods) RO 26.9.49. **12.** *30.12.57. **13.** RO (upon electrification) Mill Hill (East)—Finchley (Central) 18.5.41; Finchley (Church End) RN Finchley (Central). **14.** Service withdrawn after opening of Highgate (LPTB). High Barnet—East Finchley service operated from 14.4.40 by LPTB.

Station or line	Ownership at Closure	Pre-Group Company	Date Closed	Map Ref	Note
Fairfield Halt	LMS	LNW	11 9 39	15A3✠	
Fairford—Yarnton	WR	GW	18 6 62	9F5	1
Falkland Road	ScR	NB	15 9 58	34G5	
Fallowfield	LMR	GC	7 7 58	45A3	
Fallside	ScR	Cal.	3 8 53	44C3	
Fangfoss	NER	NE	5 1 59	22C5	
Faringdon—Uffington	WR	GW	31 12 51	10F5	5
Farington	LMR	NUJ	7 3 60	24E3	
Farlington Halt	SRy	SRy	4 7 37	4E2	
Farnell Road	ScR	Cal.	11 6 56	34C3	
Farnham (Farnham Jn)— Wanborough (Ash Jn)	SRy	LSW	4 7 37	4B1	2
Farnley & Wortley	NER	LNW	3 11 52	42A3	
Farthinghoe	LMR	LNW	3 11 52	10C4	
Farthinghoe (Cockley Brake Jn)—**Towcester**	LMR	SMJ	2 7 51	10C4	3

F

Station or line	Ownership at Closure	Pre-Group Company	Date Closed	Map Ref	Note
Felin Fran—Swansea (High Street) (Hafod Jn)	WR	GW	11 6 56	43F2	
Felin Fran (Lonlas Jn)—**Skewen** (East Jn)	WR	GW	11 6 56	43F2	
Felixstowe (Pier)—Felixstowe (Beach)	ER	GE	2 7 51	12E3	4
Fenchurch Street (Burdett Rd Jn)—**Stratford** (Bow Jn)	ER	GE	7 11 49	40C4	
Fenton	LMR	NS	6 2 61	15C3	
Ferryhill—West Hartlepool (Cemetry North Jn)	NER	NE	9 6 52	28D5	
Fersit Halt	LNE	—	31 12 34	32C1✠	
Fidler's Ferry & Penketh	LMR	LNW	2 1 50	20C3	
Finchley Road	LMS	Mid.	11 7 27	39B5	
Finningley	ER	GN&GE	11 9 61	21F5	
Finmere	LMR	GC	4 3 63	10D3	
Fishponds (Kingswood Jn)—**Montpelier** (Ashley Hill Jn)	LMS	Mid.	31 3 41	8C1	
Five Ways	LMR	Mid.	– 11 50	15G4✠	11
Flax Bourton	WR	GW	2 12 63	3A2	
Flaxton	LNE	NE	22 9 30	21B5	
Flecknoe	LMR	LNW	3 11 52	10B4	
Floriston	LMR	Cal.	17 7 50	26B1	
Flushdyke	LNE	GN	5 5 41	42C3	
Fochabers (Town)—Orbliston Junction	LMS	HR	14 9 31	36C1	
Fockerby—Reedness Junction	AJ	AJ	17 7 33	22E5	
Foggathorpe	NER	NE	20 9 54	22D5	
Ford	LMR	LY	2 4 51	45F3	
Ford Bridge	WR	S&H	5 4 54	9B1	
Fordoun	ScR	Cal.	11 6 56	34B2	
Forest Hall	NER	NE	15 9 58	27B5	
Forest Mill	LNE	NE	22 9 30	30A4	
Forgandenny	ScR	Cal.	11 6 56	33F5	
Forncett—Wymondham	LNE	GE	7 9 39	12A3	12
Forrestfield	LNE	NB	22 9 30	30C5	
Fort Augustus—Spean Bridge	LNE	NB	1 12 33	32A1	6
Forteviot	ScR	Cal.	11 6 56	33F4	
Fort George—Gollanfield Jn	LMS	HR	14 9 31	36D4	7
Fort Gomer Halt	SRy	LSW	1 5 30	4E3	
Fortrose—Muir of Ord	ScR	HR	1 10 51	36D5	8
Foryd	LMS	LNW	5 1 31	19C5	9
Fotherby Halt	ER	GN	11 9 61	17A3	
Foulis	ScR	HR	13 6 60	36C5	
Foulridge	LMR	Mid.	5 1 59	21B1	
Four Ashes	LMR	LNW	15 6 59	15E3	
Fowey—St. Blazey	GW	GW	8 7 29	1D3	
Framlingham—Wickham Market	ER	GE	3 11 52	12C3	
French Drove & Gedney Hill	ER	GN&GE	11 9 61	17F3	
Freshwater—Newport	SR	FYN	21 9 53	4F4	*
Frickley	NER	SK	10 8 53	42D1	

ABOVE: *A train of the Corris Railway.* [COURTESY W. E. HAYWARD

BELOW: *Class 5 2-6-0 No. 42796 waits at Chatburn on the Hellifield—Blackburn line on August 25, 1962.* [W. G. SUMNER

ABOVE: *Former Highland 0-4-4T No. 55051 stands at Dornoch with the branch train for The Mound.* [L. A. DENCH

BELOW: *Easingwold Railway 0-6-0ST No. 2 and a former North Eastern Railway six-wheel brake composite coach stand at Easingwold on June 30, 1933.* [H. C. CASSERLEY

ABOVE: *L.M.S. Class 3F 0-6-0T No. 16416 waits to leave Fort George with the branch train to Gollanfield Junction in May, 1928.*   [H. C. CASSERLEY

BELOW: *G.W. 0-6-0PT No. 7411 arrives at Lechlade with an Oxford—Fairford train in July 1958.*   [E. WILMSHURST

ABOVE: *Former Highland Railway 4-4-0 No. 14274 stands at Fochabers Town in May, 1930.*
[H. C. CASSERLEY

BELOW: *Former L.C.D. Class R1 0-4-4T No. 31671 at Hythe with the branch train to Sandling Junction.*
[A. W. BURGES

ABOVE: *L.M.S. Class 3F 0-6-0T No. 16415 at Hopeman station on the Highland branch from Alves in 1928.* [H. C. CASSERLEY

BELOW: *Class H 0-4-4T No. 31327 propels the Hawkhurst branch train out of Goudhurst towards Paddock Wood on April 12, 1958.* [G. DANIELS

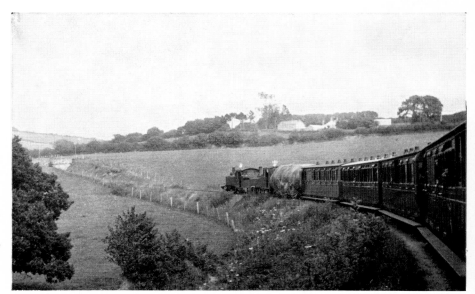

ABOVE: *Lynton & Barnstaple engines* LYN *and* EXE *double-head a train for Lynton on July 21,* *1925.* [H. C. CASSERLEY

BELOW: *Leek & Manifold Valley train at Waterhouses on April 29, 1933.* [H. C. CASSERLEY

Station or line	Ownership at Closure	Pre-Group Company	Date Closed	Map Ref	Note
Frisby	LMR	Mid.	3 7 61	16E3	
Frocester	WR	Mid.	11 12 61	9E3	
Fullerton Junction—					
Hurstbourne	SRy	LSW	6 7 31	4C4	10
Furness Abbey	LMR	Fur.	25 9 50	24B5	
Fushiebridge	LNE	NB	4 10 43	30C2	

1. Fairford—Witney*.   2. Farnham Jn—Tongham*; Tongham—Ash Jn* 2.1.61.   3. *29.10.51.   4. Cl. 11.9.39, RO 3.6.46.   5. *1.7.63.   6. *1.1.47.   7. *11.8.58.   8. *13.6.60. 9. RO as Kinmel Bay Halt 4.6.38 q.v.   10. Fullerton Jn—Longparish* 28.5.56; Longparish—Hurstbourne* 28.5.34.   11. PC. TC 2.10.44.   12. *4.8.51.

Station or line	Ownership at Closure	Pre-Group Company	Date Closed	Map Ref	Note
Gailey	LMR	LNW	18 6 51	15E3	
Galgate	LMS	LNW	1 5 39	24C3	
Gallions—Custom House	PLA	PLA	8 9 40	40C1	*
Garsdale—Northallerton:					
Garsdale—Hawes	NER	Mid.	16 3 59	27G2	*
Hawes—Northallerton	NER	NE	26 4 54	27G3	6
Garnkirk	ScR	Cal.	7 3 60	44C4	
Garston Dock—Allerton	LMS	LNW	16 6 47	45E4	1
Gartcosh	ScR	Cal.	5 11 62	44C4	
Gartmore	ScR	NB	2 1 50	29A4	
Gartsherrie	LMS	Cal.	28 10 40	44B4	
Garton	NER	NE	5 6 50	22C4	
Gatehouse of Fleet	ScR	PPW	5 12 49	25C5	2
Gatwick Airport	SR	—	27 5 58	5D3⊁	3
Geddington	LMR	Mid.	1 11 48	16G2	
Georgetown	ScR	—	2 2 59	44G4⊁	
Gifford—Smeaton Junction	LNE	NB	3 4 33	31C1	4
Gildersome	NER	GN	13 6 55	42B3	
Gilfach Goch—Blackmill	GW	GW	22 9 30	43D3	5
Gillett's Crossing Halt	LMS	PWY	11 9 39	24D4	
Gilling—Malton					
(Scarborough Road Jn)	LNE	NE	1 1 31	21A5	
Gilnockie	ScR	NB	5 1 53	26B1	
Girtford Halt	LMS	—	17 11 40	11D1⊁	
Gladstone Dock—Linacre Rd.	LMS	LY	7 7 24	45F3⊁	
Glamis	ScR	Cal.	11 6 56	34D5	
Glanrhyd Halt	WR	VT	7 3 55	14G5	
Glasgow Green	ScR	Cal.	2 11 53	44D3	
Glassaugh	ScR	GNS	21 9 53	37C2	
Glasson Dock—Lancaster					
(Castle)	LMS	LNW	7 7 30	24C3	
Glasterlaw	ScR	Cal.	2 4 51	34D3	

Station or line	Ownership at Closure	Pre-Group Company	Date Closed	Map Ref	Note
Glastonbury & Street—Wells (Priory Road)	WR	SD	29 10 51	8E2	*
Glazebury	LMR	LNW	7 7 58	45C3	
Glenboig	ScR	Cal.	11 6 56	44B4	
Glenbuck	ScR	Cal.	4 8 52	30E5	
Glencarse	ScR	Cal.	11 6 56	33F5	
Glencorse—Millerhill	LNE	NB	1 5 33	30C2	7
Glendon & Rushton	LMR	Mid.	4 1 60	10A2	
Gloucester (Central) (Over Jn)—Ledbury	WR	GW	13 7 59	9E3	8
Glyncorrwg—Cymmer Corr wg	GW	SWM	22 9 30	43E2	
Glyntaff Halt	GW	AD	5 5 30	43C3	
Godley—Woodley (Apethorne Jn)	LMR	CLC	9 9 63	21G1	
Gogar	LNE	NB	22 9 30	30B3	
Golborne (South)	LMR	LNW	6 2 61	45D3	
Golden Hill Platform	GW	GW	5 2 40	7D2	
Goldsborough	NER	NE	15 9 58	21C4	
Gomersal	NER	LNW	5 10 53	42B4	
Goole (Marshland Jn)—Haxey Junction	AJ	AJ	17 7 33	22E5	9
Gorbals	LMS	GBK	1 6 28	44E3	
Gorleston (North)	NSJ	NSJ	5 10 42	18F1	
Gosberton	ER	GN&GE	11 9 61	17D2	
Gospel Oak—Junction Road	THJ	THJ	2 11 25	40C1	
Gosport—Fareham	SR	LSW	8 6 53	4E2	
Goswick	NER	NE	15 9 58	31D4	
Gotherington Halt	WR	GW	13 6 55	9D4	
Govan—Ibrox	G&P	G&P	9 6 21	44E4	
Goxhill—Immingham Dock	ER	GC	17 6 63	22E3	16
Grain Crossing Halt	SR	SEC	3 9 51	6B4	15
Grange—Knock (Grange North Jn)	ScR	GNS	7 3 60	37D1	*
Granton—Powderhall (Bonnington South Jn)	LNE	NB	2 11 25	30F2	
Grassington—Skipton (Embsay Junction)	LMS	Mid.	22 9 30	21B1	
Grassmoor	LNE	GC	28 10 40	41C2	
Grateley—Newton Tony	SR	LSW	30 6 52	4C5	10
Gravesend (West)—Farningham Road (Fawkham Jn)	SR	SEC	3 8 53	5B5	
Grayrigg	LMR	LNW	1 2 54	27G1	
Great Bridgeford	LMR	LNW	8 8 49	20G1	
Great Glen	LMR	Mid.	18 6 51	16F3	
Great Haywood Halt	LMS	NS	6 1 47	15E4	
Great Longstone	LMR	Mid.	10 9 62	15B5	11
Great Ponton	ER	GN	15 9 58	16D1	
Greenfield—Oldham (Clegg Street)	LMR	LNW	2 5 55	21F1	
Greenloaning	ScR	Cal.	11 6 56	33G3	

Station or line	Ownership at Closure	Pre-Group Company	Date Closed			Map Ref	Note
Greenock (Princes Pier)—							
Kilmacolm	ScR	GSW	2	2	59	29B3	
Greenodd	LMS	Fur.	30	9	46	24A4	12
Greetland	NER	LY	10	9	62	42C5	
Gresford Halt (for Llay)	WR	GW	12	9	60	20E4	
Gretna	LMR	Cal.	10	9	51	26B1	
Gretton Halt	WR	GW	7	3	60	9D4	
Griffith's Crossing Halt	LMS	LNW	5	7	37	19D2	
Grimsby—Immingham							
(Tramway):							
Cleveland Bridge—							
Corporation Bridge	ER	GC	1	7	56	22F2	*
Corporation Bridge—							
Immingham	ER	GC	3	7	61	22F2	*
Grimston	LMR	Mid.	4	2	57	16E3	
Grinkle	LNE	NE	11	9	39	28E3	
Gristhorpe	NER	NE	16	2	59	22A3	
Grovesend	LMS	LNW	6	6	32	7B3	
Guay	ScR	HR	3	8	59	33D4	
Guide Bridge (Stockport Jn)—							
Oldham (Clegg Street)	LMR	OAGB	4	5	59	21F1	
Gullane—Longniddry							
(Aberlady Junction)	LNE	NB	12	9	32	30B1	13
Gunnersbury (Brentford Road							
Jn)—**Kew Bridge** (Chiswick							
Jn)	SRy	LSW	9	5	32	39D3	14
Guyhirne	ER	GN&GE	5	10	53	17F3	
Gwaen-Cae-Gurwen—							
Garnant	GW	GW	4	5	26	43F1	

1. Cl. 15.4.17 RO 5.5.19. **2.** RO 20.5.50. **3.** Station closed and the original Gatwick Racecourse station rebuilt and re-opened as the new Gatwick Airport. **4.** Gifford—Humbie* –.8.48 (Floods); Humbie—Saltoun* 2.5.60. **5.** Cl. 5.3.28; RO 26.3.28; Gilfach Goch—Hendreforganø; Hendreforgan—Blackmill* –.–.57. **6.** Hawes—Redmire *27.4.64. **7.** Glencorse—Roslin Colliery* 1.7.59. **8.** Dymock—Ledbury*, Dymock—Over Jn*1.6.64. **9.** Epworth—Haxey Jn* 1.2.56. **10.** *4.3.63. **11.** One train (Sats. excepted and unadvertised) stops for a nurse of Buxton hospital after protest at closure. **12.** Cl. 16.9.40 RO 3.6.46. Officially cl. 13.6.55 but trains did not stop after 29.9.46. **13.** *15.6.64. **14.** *1.7.32. **15.** Replaced by new station (Grain) immediately east of old, for oil refinery. **16.** Goxhill—Admiralty Siding*.

Station or line	Ownership at Closure	Pre-Group Company	Date Closed			Map Ref	Note
Haddenham	WR	GW&GC	7	1	63	10E3	
Haddington—Longniddry	ScR	NB	5	12	49	30B1	
Hadleigh—Bentley	LNE	GE	29	2	32	12D4	
Hadnall	LMR	LNW	2	5	60	15E1	
Haggerston	LMS	NL	6	5	40	40B4	

Station or line	Ownership at Closure	Pre-Group Company	Date Closed			Map Ref	Note
Hainton Street Halt	ER	GN	11	9	61	22F2	
Halbeath	LNE	NB	22	9	30	30A3	
Halebank	LMR	LNW	15	9	58	45E4	1
Halewood	LMR	CLC	17	9	51	45E4	
Halewood (**East Jn—North Jn**)	LMR	CLC	7	11	60	45E4	
Halifax (Town)—Bradford (Exchange) via Queensbury	NER	GN	23	5	55	42B5	25
Halkirk	ScR	HR	13	6	60	38D3	
Hallatrow—Limpley Stoke	GW	GW	21	9	25	3B3	2
Halton (Lancs)	LMR	Mid.	7	7	52	45D5	
Hambleton	NER	NE	14	9	59	21D5	
Hamilton—Shettleston:							
Hamilton—Bothwell	ScR	NB	15	9	52	44B2	*3
Bothwell—Shettleston	ScR	NB	4	7	55	44C3	24
Hamilton (West) (Strathaven Jn)—**High Blantyre** (Auchenraith Jn)	LMS	Cal.	1	10	45	44B2	
Hampole	NER	WRG	7	1	52	21F4	
Hampsthwaite	NER	NE	2	1	50	21C3	
Handsworth Wood	LMS	LNW	5	5	41	13B3	
Hanwood	WR	SWP	12	9	60	14A1	
Harborne—Monument Lane (Harborne Jn)	LMS	LNW	26	11	34	13C3	4
Hare Park & Crofton	NER	WRG	31	3	52	42C2	
Hare Park & Crofton (Nostell North Jn)—**Stairfoot** (Old Oak Jn)	LNE	GC	22	9	30	42D2	
Harker	LNE	NB	1	11	29	26C1	
Harmston	ER	GN	10	9	62	16B1	
Harringworth	LMR	Mid.	1	11	48	16F1	
Harston	ER	GE	17	6	63	11D3	
Hart	NER	NE	31	8	53	28D4	8
Hartshill & Basford Halt	LMS	NS	20	9	26	15C3✠	
Haslingden	LMR	LY	7	11	60	20A1	
Hassop	LMS	Mid.	17	8	42	15B5	
Hathern	LMR	Mid.	4	1	60	16D4	
Haughton	LMR	LNW	23	5	49	20G1	
Haverhill (South)	LNE	CVH	14	7	24	11D5	
Haverthwaite	LMS	Fur.	30	9	46	24A4	7
Hawkhurst—Paddock Wood	SR	SEC	12	6	61	6E5	*
Haxby	LNE	NE	22	9	30	21C5	
Haxey & Epworth	ER	GN&GE	2	2	59	22F5	
Hay—Pontrilas	GW	GW	15	12	41	14F1	26
Hayles Abbey Halt	WR	GW	7	3	60	9D4	
Hayling Island—Havant	SR	LBSC	4	11	63	4E2	*
Hazlehead Bridge	ER	GC	6	3	50	42E4	
Heacham—Wells-on-Sea	ER	GE	2	6	52	17D5	9
Headcorn—Robertsbridge	SR	KES	4	1	54	6D5	10
Heanor—Ilkeston (Stanton Junction)	LNE	GN	4	12	39	41F3	27
Heath	ER	GC	4	3	63	41C3	

Station or line	Ownership at Closure	Pre-Group Company	Date Closed	Map Ref	Note
Heath (Heath Jn)—**Staveley (Central)** via Chesterfield	ER	GC	4 3 63	41C3	12
Heath Park Halt—Harpenden (Harpenden Jn)	LMS	Mid.	16 6 47	11F1	11
Heaton Mersey	LMR	Mid.	3 7 61	45A4	
Heaton Norris	LMR	LNW	2 3 59	45A3	
Heck	NER	NE	15 9 58	21E5	
Heckmondwike (Spen)	NER	LNW	5 10 53	42C4	
Heckmondwike (Central)— Thornhill	NER	LY	1 1 62	42C4	
Heddon-on-the-Wall Halt	NER	NE	15 9 58	27B5	
Hellesdon	ER	MGN	15 9 52	18F3	
Helmdon	LMR	GC	4 3 63	10C3	
Helpringham	ER	GN&GE	4 7 55	17D1	
Helston—Gwinear Road	WR	GW	5 11 62	1F5	
Hemyock—Tiverton Junction	WR	GW	9 9 63	2A2	
Hereford—Three Cocks Jn	WR	Mid.	31 12 62	9C1	13
Hertford (North) (Old)— **Hertford (North)** (New)	LNE	GN	2 6 24	11F2	
Hertford (North)—Stevenage (Langley Jn)	LNE	GN	10 9 39	11F2	14
Hertford (North)—Welwyn Garden City	ER	GN	18 6 51	11F2	
Heslerton	LNE	NE	22 9 30	22A4	
Hessay	NER	NE	15 9 58	21C4	
Hexham (Border Counties Jn)— **Riccarton Jn**	NER	NB	15 10 56	27B3	15
Hey's Crossing Halt	LMR	LY	18 6 51	45E2	
Heytesbury	SR	GW	19 9 55	3C4	
Higham Ferrers— Wellingborough (Midland Road) (Irchester Jn)	LMR	Mid.	15 6 59	10A1	
High Field	NER	NE	20 9 54	22D5	
High Rocks Halt	SR	LBSC	5 5 52	5D5	
High Westwood	LNE	NE	4 5 42	27C4	
Highworth—Swindon (Highworth Junction)	WR	GW	2 3 53	9F5	16
Hilgay	ER	GE	4 11 63	11A4	
Hillside	LNE	NB	– 2 27	34C2	
Hilton House	LMR	LY	1 2 54	45C2	
Hindley Green	LMR	LNW	1 5 61	45C2	
Hipperholme	NER	LY	8 6 53	42B5	
Hirwaun (Gelli Tarw Jn)— **Merthyr** (Mardy Jn)	WR	GW	31 12 62	43D2	
Hixton Halt	LMS	NS	6 1 47	15D4	
Hoghton	LMR	LY	12 9 60	20A2	
Holbeck (High Level)	NER	GN	7 7 58	42A3	
Holbeck (Low Level)	NER	Mid.	7 7 58	42A3	
Holburn Street	LNE	GNS	5 4 37	37G4	
Holcombe Brook—Bury (Bolton Street)	LMR	LY	5 5 52	45B1	18

H

Station or line	Ownership at Closure	Pre-Group Company	Date Closed	Map Ref	Note
Holehouse—Ochiltree (Belston Junction)	ScR	GSW	3 4 50	29F4	
Holehouse Junction	ScR	GSW	3 4 50	29F4	
Holland Arms	LMR	LNW	4 8 52	19D1	
Holland Road Halt	SR	LBSC	7 5 56	5F3	
Holme	ER	GN	6 4 59	11A2	
Holme	LMS	LY	28 7 30	24D1✠	
Holme Moor	NER	NE	20 9 54	22D5	
Holmes	ER	Mid.	19 9 55	42F1	
Holmfirth—Brockholes	NER	LY	2 11 59	42D5	
Holtby	LNE	NE	11 9 39	21C5	
Holton-le-Clay	ER	GN	4 7 55	22F2	
Holton Village Halt	ER	GN	11 9 61	22F2	
Holytown (Cleland Jn)— **Morningside** via Newmains	LMS	Cal.	1 12 30	30C5	
Holywell (Town)—Holywell Junction	LMR	LNW	6 9 54	20D5	19
Holywood	ScR	GSW	26 9 49	26A4	
Honeybourne **(West Loop— North Loop)**	WR	GW	7 3 60	9C5	
Honington	ER	GN	10 9 62	16C1	
Hooton—West Kirby	LMR	BJ	17 9 56	20D4	20
Hope (Exchange) (High Level)	LMR	GC	1 9 58	20E4	
Hope (Exchange) (Low Level)	LMR	LNW	1 9 58	20E4	
Hopeman—Alves	LMS	HR	14 9 31	36C2	21
Hopperton	NER	—	15 9 58	21C4✠	
Horbury (Millfield Road)	NER	LY	6 11 61	42C2	
Hornby	LMR	Mid.	16 9 57	24B2	
Horncastle—Woodhall Jn	ER	GN	13 9 54	17B2	
Horninglow	LMR	NS	1 1 49	15C5	
Hornsey Road	THJ	THJ	3 5 43	40B5	
Horsted Keynes—Haywards Heath (Copyhold Jn)	SR	LBSC	28 10 63	5E3	28
Horton Park	NER	GN	15 9 52	42B5	
Hothfield Halt	SR	SEC	2 11 59	6D4	
Hotwells—Sea Mills (Sneyd Park Jn)	GW&Mid.	GW&Mid.	2 7 22	3G1	*
Hougham	ER	GN	16 9 57	16C1	
Houghton Halt	WR	GW	12 9 60	20G4	
Howden Clough	NER	GN	1 12 52	42B3	
Howe Bridge	LMR	LNW	20 7 59	45C2	
How Mill	NER	NE	5 1 59	27C1	
Howwood	ScR	GSW	7 3 55	29C4	
Hucknall (Central)	LMR	GC	4 3 63	41E4	
Hullavington	WR	GW	3 4 61	9G3	
Hull (Cannon St)—Willerby & Kirk Ella (Springbank Jn)	LNE	HB	14 7 24	22A1	22
Hundred End	LMR	LY	30 4 62	24E3	
Hunslet	NER	Mid.	13 6 60	42B2	
Hurdlow	LMR	LNW	15 8 49	15B5	
Hurlford	ScR	GSW	7 3 55	29E4	
Husborne Crawley Halt	LMS	LNW	5 5 41	10C1	

Station or line	Ownership at Closure	Pre-Group Company	Date Closed	Map Ref	Note
Hutcheon Street	LNE	GNS	5 4 37	37F4	
Hutton Gate—Whitby (West Cliff):					
Hutton Gate (Hutton Jn)—					
Loftus	NER	NE	2 5 60	28E3	17
Loftus—Whitby (West Cliff)	NER	NE	5 5 58	28E3	*
Huttons Ambo	LNE	NE	22 9 30	22B5	
Huyton Quarry	LMR	LNW	15 9 58	45E4	
Hyde Road	LMR	GC	7 7 58	45A3	
Hyndland—Partick Hill	ScR	NB	6 11 60	44E4	23

1. Cl. 1.1.17 RO 5.5.19. **2.** Cl. 22.3.15 RO 9.7.23. Hallatrow—Camerton*; Camerton—Limpley Stoke* 15.2.51. **3.** Hamilton—New connection with ex. Cal. Cadzow Colliery branchø. **4.** *4.11.63.
7. Cl. 16.9.40 RO 3.6.46. Officially cl. 13.6.55 but trains did not stop after 29.9.46. **8.** Cl. 28.7.41 RO 6.5.46. **9.** Burnham Market—Wells-on-Sea* 31.3.53, after floods. **10.** Headcorn—Tenterden Town*; Tenterden Town—Robertsbridge* 12.6.61. **11.** Heath Park Halt—Hemel Hempstead* 31.8.59; Hemel Hempstead—Claydale Sidings* 1.7.63. **12.** Heath Jn—Chesterfield (Hydes Works)* 17.6.63; Sheepbridge—Staveley Works* 12.8.63. **13.** Hay-on-Wye—Three Cocks Jn*. **14.** RO 5.3.62. **15.** Hexham—Reedsmouth, Bellingham—Riccarton Jn* 1.9.58; Reedsmouth—Bellingham* 11.11.63. **16.** Highworth—Kingsdown Road Box (between Stanton and Stratton)* 6.8.62. **17.** Hutton Jn—Boosbeck*; Boosbeck—Brotton Jn* –.–.63. **18.** Holcombe Brook—Tottington* 2.5.60; Tottington—Bury (B. St.)* 19.8.63. **19.** Holywell Town—Crescent Sdg.*; Crescent Sdg.—Holywell Jn* 11.8.57. **20.** *7.5.62. **21.** Hopeman—Burghead* 30.12.57. **22.** Trains diverted to Paragon station. **23.** New Hyndland station opened 1000 yards west of Partick Hill. **24.** Bothwell—Mount Vernonø. **25.** Halifax (North Bridge)—Holmfield* 27.6.60; Holmfield—Queensbury* 18.5.56. **26.** Hay—Dorstone* 2.1.50; Dorstone—Abbeydore* 2.2.53. **27.** Cl. 30.4.28 RO 2.10.39; Heanor—Nutbrook Sdgs.* 7.10.63; Nutbrook Sdgs.—Stanton Jn* 16.12.63. **28.** Horsted Keynes—Ardingly*.

Station or line	Ownership at Closure	Pre-Group Company	Date Closed	Map Ref	Note
Icknield Port Road	LMS	LNW	18 5 31	13C3	
Ilford—Newbury Park	LNE	GE	30 11 47	40B1	*
Ilkeston (Town)—Ilkeston Junction & Cossall (Ilkeston South Jn)	LMS	Mid.	16 6 47	41F3	
Ilkeston (**West Jn—Bonnesley Jn**)	LMS	Mid.	16 6 47	41F3	
Ilmer Halt	WR	—	7 1 63	10E2✠	
Inchture	ScR	Cal.	11 6 56	34E5	
Innerwick	ScR	NB	18 6 51	31B2	
Inveramsay	ScR	GNS	1 10 51	37E3	
Inverbervie—Montrose (Broomfield Jn)	ScR	NB	1 10 51	34C2	

Station or line	Ownership at Closure	Pre-Group Company	Date Closed	Map Ref	Note
Inverkeilor	LNE	NB	22 9 30	34D3	
Irchester	LMR	Mid.	7 3 60	10B1	
Irlams-o'th'-Height	LMR	LY	5 3 56	45B2	
Irvine—Kilwinning	LMS	Cal.	28 7 30	29E3	1
Ivybridge	WR	GW	2 3 59	2D5	

1. *1.6.39.

Station or line	Ownership at Closure	Pre-Group Company	Date Closed	Map Ref	Note
Jackaments Bridge Halt	WR	—	27 9 48	9F4✠	
Jedburgh—Roxburgh	ScR	NB	12 8 48	31E1	1
Johnstone (North)	ScR	GSW	7 3 55	29C4	
Johnstown & Hafod Halt	WR	GW	12 9 60	20F4	
Junction Road	THJ	THJ	3 5 43	40B5	

1. Cl. by floods. RO to freight 26.8.48.

Station or line	Ownership at Closure	Pre-Group Company	Date Closed	Map Ref	Note
Keighley (Ingrow GN Jn)— **Queensbury**	NER	GN	23 5 55	21D2	10
Keinton Mandeville	WR	GW	10 9 62	8F2	
Kelston	LMR	Mid.	1 1 49	8D1	
Kelty	LNE	NB	22 9 30	30A3	
Kelvinbridge	ScR	Cal.	4 8 52	44E4	
Kelvinside	LMS	Cal.	1 7 42	44E4	
Kemp Town—London Road (B'ton) (Kemp Town Jn)	SRy	LBSC	2 1 33	5F3	
Kempston & Elstow Halt	LMS	LNW	5 5 41	11D1	
Kenfig Hill	WR	GW	5 5 58	43E4	
Kensington (Addison Road)—Clapham Junction	WLE	WLE	21 10 40	39D4	1
Kensington (Uxbridge Rd. Jn— Latimer Road)	Met.&GW	Met.&GW	20 10 40	39D4	2
Kenyon Junction	LMR	LNW	2 1 61	45C3	
Kerry—Abermule	GW	GW	9 2 31	14C2	3
Kettering (Kettering Jn)—**St. Ives**	LMR/ER	Mid.	15 6 59	10A2	4
Kew Bridge—South Acton (Bollo Lane Jn)	NSW	NSW	12 9 40	39D3	

ABOVE: *Former Highland 4-4-0T No. 15013 waits at Lybster with the branch train to Wick on May 19, 1928.* [H. C. CASSERLEY

BELOW: *L.B.S.C.R. "Terrier" 0-6-0T No. 661 at Lee-on-the-Solent with the branch train for Fort Brockhurst.* [H. C. CASSERLEY

C**

ABOVE: *The last train from Tredegar arrives at Nantybwch on June 11, 1960.* [E. WILMSHURST

BELOW: *An auto train from Merthyr to Abergavenny Junction arrives at Rhymney Bridge on September 30, 1957.* [G. DANIELS

Station or line	Ownership at Closure	Pre-Group Company	Date Closed	Map Ref	Note
Kidsgrove (Market Street) Halt	LMR	NS	25 9 50	15C3	
Kidwelly Flats Halt	WR	—	11 11 57	7A2✠	
Kilbirnie—Giffen	LMS	Cal.	1 12 30	29D3	*
Kildary	ScR	HR	13 6 60	36C4	
Killamarsh (Central)	ER	GC	4 3 63	41A3	
Killamarsh (West)	ER	Mid.	1 2 54	41A3	
Killingworth	NER	NE	15 9 58	27B5	
Killochan	ScR	GSW	1 1 51	29G3	
Killywhan	ScR	GSW	3 8 59	26B4	
Kilsby & Crick	LMR	LNW	1 2 60	10A4	
Kinbuck	ScR	Cal.	11 6 56	33G3	
Kinfauns	ScR	Cal.	2 1 50	33F5	
Kingham—Kings Sutton:					
Kingham—Chipping Norton	WR	GW	3 12 62	9D5	
Chipping Norton—Kings Sutton	WR	GW	4 6 51	10D5	9
Kingsbarns	LNE	NB	22 9 30	34F3	
Kingsbridge—Brent	WR	GW	16 9 63	2E4	*
King's Cross (Met)	LPTB	Met.	16 10 40	40C5	11
King's Lynn (Harbour Jn)—South Lynn	ER	MGN	2 3 59	17E4	
Kinniel	LNE	NB	22 9 30	30B4	
Kinmel Bay Halt	LMS	—	2 9 39	19C5✠	12
Kirby Park	LMR	BJ	5 7 54	20C5	
Kirkburton—Deighton (Kirkburton Jn)	LMS	LNW	28 7 30	21E2	
Kirkby Bentinck	LMR	GC	4 3 63	41E4	
Kirkby-in-Ashfield—Pye Bridge	LMR	Mid.	10 9 51	41E4	6
Kirkby Stephen (East)—Tebay	LMR	NE	1 12 52	27F2	5
Kirkby Thore	LMR	NE	7 12 53	27E2	
Kirkgunzeon	ScR	GSW	2 1 50	26B4	
Kirkham Abbey	LNE	NE	22 9 30	22B5	
Kirklee	LMS	Cal.	1 5 39	44E4	
Kirkpatrick	ScR	Cal.	13 6 60	26B2	
Kirriemuir—Forfar (Kirriemuir Jn)	ScR	Cal.	4 8 52	34D4	
Kirtlebridge	ScR	Cal.	13 6 60	26B2	
Kirton	ER	GN	11 9 61	17D2	
Knapton	LNE	NE	22 9 30	22B4	
Knaresborough—Pilmoor	NER	NE	25 9 50	21C3	7
Knott End—Garstang & Catterall	LMS	KE	31 3 30	24C4	8
Knutton Halt	LMS	NS	20 9 26	20F1✠	

1. Workmen's service still operated. **2.** Cl. by bomb damage. *1.2.60. **3.** *1.5.56. **4.** Kimbolton—Huntingdon, Godmanchester—St. Ives*; Huntingdon—Godmanchester* 4.6.60; Kimbolton—Cranford* 28.10.63. **5.** *22.1.62. **6.** PC. TC 16.6.47. **7.** Brafferton—Pilmoor* 1.3.52. **8.** Knott End—Pilling* 13.11.50; Pilling—Garstang Town* 31.7.63. **9.** Chipping Norton—Great Rollright siding* 3.12.62; Great Rollright siding—Hook Norton* (Landslip) –.8.59; Hook Norton—Adderbury* 4.11.63. **10.** Ingrow (GN Jn)—Ingrow (East)* 18.6.62; Ingrow (East)—Cullingworth*; Cullingworth—Thornton* 11.11.63. **11.** Bomb damage. New station opened 14.3.41. **12.** Formerly Foryd q.v.; Cl. 10.9.38, RO 19.6.39.

L

Station or line	Ownership at Closure	Pre- Group Company	Date Closed			Map Ref	Note
Ladybank—Mawcarse Jn	ScR	NB	5	6	50	34F5	30
Lakeside—Ulverston							
(Plumpton Jn)	LMR	Fur.	13	6	55	24A4	28
Lambourn—Newbury	WR	GW	4	1	60	4A4	1
Lamesley	LNE	NE	4	6	45	27C5	
Langho	LMR	LY	7	5	56	24D2	
Langport (East)	WR	GW	10	9	62	8F3	
Langwith Junction—							
Beighton (Killamarsh Jn)	LNE	GC	10	9	39	41C4	2
Larbert—Maryhill:							
Larbert (Larbert Jn)—							
Kilsyth (New)	LMS&LNE	Cal.&NB	1	2	35	30B5	15
Kilsyth (Kelvin Valley East							
Jn)—**Maryhill** (East Jn)	ScR	NB	2	4	51	29B5	29
Kilsyth—Kirkintilloch							
(Kelvin Valley West Jn)	ScR	NB	6	8	51	29B5	
Lauder—Fountainhall Jn	LNE	NB	12	9	32	30D1	4
Launceston (North)	WR	GW	30	6	52	1B4	24
Launceston—Plymouth							
(Tavistock Jn)	WR	GW	31	12	62	1B4	3
Laverton Halt	WR	GW	7	3	60	9C4	
Laxfield—Haughley	ER	MSL	28	7	52	12B3	*
Lea	ER	GN&GE	6	8	57	16A2	
Leadburn	ScR	NB	7	3	55	30C2	
Lea Green	LMR	LNW	7	3	55	45D3	
Leamington Spa (Avenue)—							
Rugby (Midland)	LMR	LNW	15	6	59	10B5	
Leamington Spa (Avenue)							
(Marton Jn)—**Weedon**	LMR	LNW	15	9	58	10B5	5
Leamside—Ferryhill							
(Tursdale Jn)	LNE	NE	28	7	41	28D5	
Leamside	NER	NE	5	10	53	28D5	
Lea Road	LMS	PWY	2	5	38	24D3	
Leatherhead	SRy	LSW	10	7	27	5C2	6
Leaton	WR	GW	12	9	60	15E1	
Ledsham	LMR	BJ	20	7	59	45F5	
Leebotwood Halt	WR	S&H	9	6	58	14B1	
Leeds (Marsh Lane)	NER	NE	15	9	58	42A2	
Leegate	LMR	M&C	5	6	50	26D2	
Leek—North Rode	LMR	NS	7	11	60	15C4	31
Leek (Leek Brook Jn)—							
Stoke-on-Trent (Stoke Jn)	LMR	NS	7	5	56	15C4	
Lee-on-the-Solent—Fort							
Brockhurst	SRy	LSW	1	1	31	4E3	7
Legbourne Road	ER	GN	7	12	53	17A3	
Leicester (Belgrave Road)—							
John O'Gaunt	LMR	GN	7	12	53	16F3	8
Leicester (London Road)							
(Wigston Central Jn)—**Rugby**							
(Midland)	LMR	Mid.	1	1	62	16F3	9
Leicester (West Bridge)—							
Desford	LMS	Mid.	24	9	28	16F4	

Station or line	Ownership at Closure	Pre-Group Company	Date Closed	Map Ref	Note
Leigh-on-Sea	LMS	Mid.	4 1 34	6A5	25
Leith (Central)—Abbeyhill					
(London Road Jn)	ScR	NB	7 4 52	30B2	
Leith (North)—Edinburgh					
(Princes Street) (Dalry Jn)	ScR	Cal.	30 4 62	30B2	26
Leith Walk	LNE	NB	31 3 30	30F2	
Leman Street	LNE	GE	7 7 41	40C4	
Lemington	NER	NE	15 9 58	27B5	
Lentran	ScR	HR	13 6 60	36D5	
Leominster—Bromyard	WR	GW	15 9 52	9B1	*
Leslie—Markinch	LNE	NB	4 1 32	34G5	
Letham Grange	LNE	NB	22 9 30	34D3	
Leuchars Junction—Tayport	ScR	NB	9 1 56	34F4	*27
Levenshulme (South)	LMR	GC	7 7 58	45A3	
Lewistown Halt	WR	—	4 6 51	43D3✠	
Leysdown—Queenborough	SR	SEC	4 12 50	6B3	*
Lifford	LMS	Mid.	27 11 46	9A4	10
Linacre Road	LMR	LY	2 4 51	45F3	
Lincoln (Sincil Bank Jn—					
Washingborough Jn)	ER	GN	4 6 62	16B1	*
Lindal	LMR	Fur.	1 10 51	24B4	
Lintz Green	NER	NE	2 11 53	27C5	
Lipson Vale Halt	SRy	LSW	5 4 42	1A2✠	
Little Bytham	ER	GN	15 6 59	17E1	
Little Mill	NER	NE	15 9 58	31F5	
Little Somerford	WR	GW	3 4 61	9G4	
Little Steeping	ER	GN	11 9 61	17B3	
Little Stretton Halt	WR	—	9 6 58	14B1✠	
Littleworth	ER	GN	11 9 61	17E2	
Liversedge (Spen)	NER	LNW	5 10 53	42B4	
Livingston	ScR	NB	1 11 48	30C4	
Llanberis—Caernarvon	LMS	LNW	12 9 32	19E2	11
Llandarcy Halt	GW	—	4 10 47	43F2✠	
Llandulas	LMR	LNW	1 12 52	19D4	
Llangynog—Oswestry					
(Llynclys Jn)	WR	Cam.	15 1 51	19G5	13
Llanmorlais—Gowerton	LMS	LNW	5 1 31	7B3	14
Llanrhaiadr	LMR	LNW	2 2 53	19E5	
Llantarnam	WR	GW	30 4 62	43A3	
Llantrisant (Mwyndy Jn)—					
Pontypridd (Tonteg Jn)	WR	TV	31 3 52	43C4	
Llanvihangel	WR	GW	9 6 58	14G1	
Llanwern	WR	GW	12 9 60	8B3	
Llysfaen	LMS	LNW	5 1 31	19D4	
Lochanhead	LMS	GSW	25 9 39	26B4	
Lochluichart	ScR	HR	3 5 54	35C4	16
Lochside	ScR	GSW	4 7 55	29C3	
Loch Tay—Killin	LMS	Cal.	9 9 39	33E2	*17
Lockington	NER	NE	13 6 60	22C4	
Lofthouse & Outwood	NER	GN	13 6 60	42B2	
Lofthouse-in-Nidderdale—					
Pateley Bridge	NV	NV	1 1 30	21B2	18

Station or line	Ownership at Closure	Pre- Group Company	Date Closed	Map Ref	Note
Long Ashton	GW	—	6 10 41	8D2✠	
Longford & Exhall	LMR	LNW	23 5 49	16G5	
Longforgan	ScR	Cal.	11 6 56	34E5	
Longhirst	NER	NE	29 10 51	27A5	
Longhoughton	NER	NE	18 6 62	31F5	
Longridge—Preston	LMS	PL	2 6 30	24D2	
Longsight	LMR	LNW	15 9 58	45A3	
Long Sutton & Pitney	WR	GW	10 9 62	8F2	
Lords	LPTB	Met.	20 11 39	39C5	23
Loth	ScR	HR	13 6 60	38G4	
Loughborough (Derby Road)—Shackerstone	LMS	LNW	13 4 31	16E4	20
Loughor	WR	GW	4 4 60	7B3	
Louth (Mablethorpe Jn)— **Mablethorpe**	ER	GN	5 12 60	17A3	*
Lowca—Workington (Harrington Jn)	LMS	CWJ	31 5 26	26E3	12
Lower Darwen	LMR	LY	3 11 58	24E2	
Lower Penarth Halt	WR	TV	14 6 54	43B5	
Lower Pontnewydd	WR	GW	9 6 58	43A3	
Low Fell	NER	NE	7 4 52	27C5	
Low Gill	LMR	LNW	7 3 60	27G1	
Low Row	NER	NE	5 1 59	27C1	
Lowton	LMR	LNW	26 9 49	45D3	
Lucker	NER	NE	2 2 53	31E4	
Ludborough	ER	GN	11 9 61	22G2	
Luddendenfoot	NER	LY	10 9 62	21E1	
Ludgate Hill	SRy	SEC	3 3 29	40C5	
Lunan Bay	LNE	NB	22 9 30	34D3	
Luncarty	ScR	Cal.	18 6 51	33E5	
Lybster—Wick	LMS	HR	1 4 44	38E2	*
Lydbrook Jn—Sharpness: Lydbrook Jn—Lydney (Town)	SVW	SVW	8 7 29	9E1	22
Lydney (Town)—Sharpness	WR	SVW	26 10 60	9E2	21
Lydstep Halt	WR	GW	2 1 56	7D2	
Lyneside	LNE	NB	1 11 29	26B1	

1. Lambourn—Welford Park*. **2.** Langwith Jn now called Shirebrook North. **3.** Launceston—Lifton, Tavistock (South)—Marsh Mills*. **4.** *1.10.58. **5.** Southam & Long Itchington (Rugby Cement Sdg)—Napton & Stockton* 3.12.62; Napton & Stockton—Weedon* 2.12.63. **6.** Trains used ex-LBSC station upon the opening of a new junction on same date. **7.** *30.9.35. **8.** Workmen's service operated until 8.12.56 and from 31.12.56 until 29.4.57. Excursion trains ran until 10.9.62. Humberstone—John o'Gaunt (Marefield Jn)* 1.6.64. **9.** Wigston Central Jn—Rugby Wharf*. **10.** PC. TC 30.9.40. **11.** Cl. 22.9.30 RO 18.7.32 to Llanberis, intermediate stations not being served. Summer excursions ran from 1933 until 1939 and from 1946 until the last one on 7.9.62. **12.** Mineral traffic now operated by NCB. **13.** Llangynog—Llanrhaiadr Mochnant* 1.7.52. Llanrhaiadr Mochnant —Blodwell Jn* 6.1.64. **14.** *2.9.57. **15.** Bonnywater Jn—Dennyloanheadø; Dennyloanhead —Banknock* 1.3.56; Banknock—Kilsyth Jn *4.5.64. **16.** Replaced by new station on a deviation of the line. **17.** Line retained to give access to Loch Tay loco. shed, where branch engine is based. **18.** Lofthouse-in-Nidderdale—Ramsgill*; Ramsgill—Pateley Bridge* 31.3.30. **20.** Hugglescote—Shackerstone was LNW & Mid. Jt. Loughborough (Derby Road)—Shepshed* 30.11.55; Shepshed—Hugglescote (Coalville East Jn, Whitwick Colliery)*

12.12.63. **21.** Service suspended due to damage to Severn Bridge. **22.** Lydbrook Jn—
Speech House Roadø; Speech House Road—Coleford Jn* 12.8.63. **23.** Formerly St. John's
Wood Road. **24.** Trains diverted to WR (LSW) station. **25.** New station opened, ½ mile
west of old. **26.** Coltbridge—Dalry (Middle Jn) *9.3.64. **27.** Leuchars (Old)—Tayport
Mill*. **28.** Summer excursions continue to run. **29.** Kelvin Valley East Jn—Torranceø;
Torrance—Balmore* 5.10.59; Balmore—Maryhill (East Jn)* –.–.61. **30.** Ladybank—Auch-
termuchtyø. **31.** *15.6.64.

Station or line	Ownership at Closure	Pre-Group Company	Date Closed			Map Ref	Note
Macclesfield (Hibel Road)	LMR	LNW	7	11	60	45A5	
Macduff—Inveramsay	ScR	GNS	1	10	51	37C2	1
Machen—Pontypridd (P C & N Jn)	WR	GW	17	9	56	43B3	2
Macmerry—Ormiston	LNE	NB	1	7	25	30B1	3
Madeley	LMR	LNW	4	2	52	20F1	
Madeley Road	LMS	NS	20	7	31	15C3	
Magdalen Green	ScR	Cal.	11	6	56	34E2	
Maindy Halt	WR	TV	15	9	58	43B4✠	
Maldon (East)—Woodham Ferrers	LNE	GE	10	9	39	12F5	4
Malmesbury—Little Somerford	WR	GW	10	9	51	9F3	5
Manchester (Mayfield)	LMR	LNW	28	8	60	45A3	
Mangotsfield (**North Junction— South Junction**)	WR	Mid.	10	9	62	3A3	
Mansfield (Town)—Rolleston Junction:							
Mansfield (Town) (North Jn) —Southwell	LMS	Mid.	12	8	29	16B4	
Southwell—Rolleston Junction	ER	Mid.	15	6	59	16C3	
Mansfield Woodhouse (Pleasley Jn)—**Staveley (Town)** (Seymour Jn)	LMS	Mid.	28	7	30	41D4	6
Marchington	LMR	NS	15	9	58	15D5	
Margate (East)	SR	SEC	4	5	53	6B1	
Margate (Sands)—Ramsgate (Town)	SRy	SEC	2	7	26	6B1	7
Market Drayton—Silverdale	LMR	NS	7	5	56	15D2	
Market Harborough— Northampton (Castle)	LMR	LNW	4	1	60	16G2	
Market Harborough (Welham Jn)—**Radcliffe-on-Trent** (Saxondale Jn)	LMR/ER	GN&LNW	7	12	53	16G2	8
Marlborough Road	LPTB	Met.	20	11	39	39B5	
Marlborough—Savernake	GW	GW	6	3	33	4A5	9*
Marlpool	LNE	GN	30	4	28	41F3	
Marshbrook	WR	S&H	9	6	58	14C1	
Marshfield	WR	GW	10	8	59	43A4	
Marsh Lane & Strand Road	LMS	LY	19	5	41	45F3	10
Marston Moor	NER	NE	15	9	58	21C4	

Station or line	Ownership at Closure	Pre-Group Company	Date Closed			Map Ref	Note
Maryhill (Central)—							
Stobcross via Kelvinbridge	ScR	Cal.	23	11	59	44E4	31
Marykirk	ScR	Cal.	11	6	56	34C3	
Masham—Melmerby	LNE	NE	1	1	31	21A3	11
Maxwelltown	LMS	GSW	1	3	39	26B4	
Medge Hall	ER	GC	12	9	60	22F5	
Meikle Earnock Halt	LMS	Cal.	12	12	43	44B1	
Melcombe Regis	SR	WP	14	9	59	3G3	32
Melling	LMR	FMJ	5	5	52	24B2	
Melmerby—Thirsk	NER	NE	14	9	59	21A3	*
Meltham—Lockwood	LMR	LY	23	5	49	21F2	
Melton	ER	GE	2	5	55	12D3	
Menston **(Menston Jn—**							
Milnerwood Jn)	NER	Mid.	25	2	57	21D2	
Menthorpe Gate	NER	NE	7	12	53	21D5	
Merthyr (Rhydycar Jn)—							
Ponsticill Junction	WR	LNW&BM	13	11	61	43C2	34
Merthyr (Rhydycar Jn)—							
Quaker's Yard (H.L.)	WR	QYM	12	2	51	43C2	22
Merton Park—Tooting		LBSC&					
Junction	SRy	LSW	3	3	29	39F4	26
Methil—Thornton Junction	ScR	NB	10	1	55	30A2	27
Methley Junction	LMS	LY	4	10	43	42B1	
Methley (North)	NER	Mid.	16	9	57	42B1	
Methley (South)	NER	MJ	7	3	60	42B1	
Methven—Methven Junction	LMS	Cal.	27	9	37	33E4	
Mexborough (West Jn)—							
Penistone (Barnsley Jn)	ER	GC	29	6	59	21F4	
Mickleton Halt	GW	—	6	10	41	9C4/5✠	
Mickle Trafford	LMR	BJ	2	4	51	20D3	
Mickle Trafford	LMR	CLC	12	2	51	20D3	
Middleton Junction—Oldham							
(Werneth)	LMR	LY	7	1	63	45A2	14
Middleton-on-Lune	LMS	LNW	13	4	31	24A2	
Middleton-on-the-Wolds	NER	NE	20	9	54	22C4	
Middlewood (Higher)	LMR	GC&NS	7	11	60	15A4	
Midge Hall	LMR	LY	2	10	61	24E3	
Midhurst	SRy	LSW	13	7	25	4D1	33
Mildenhall—Cambridge							
(Barnwell Jn)	ER	GE	18	6	62	11B5	15
Mildmay Park	LMS	NL	1	10	34	40B4	
Milford & Brocton	LMR	LNW	6	3	50	15E4	
Millerhill	ScR	NB	7	11	55	30B2	
Millfield	NER	NE	2	5	55	28C5	
Milltimber	LNE	GNS	5	4	37	37G3	
Milton Range Halt	SRy	SEC	17	7	32	5B5✠	
Minshull Vernon	LMS	LNW	2	3	42	20E2	
Minsterley—Hanwood							
(Cruckmeole Jn)	WR	SWP	5	2	51	14B1	
Misterton	ER	GN&GE	11	9	61	22G5	
Moat Lane Junction—							
Talyllyn Junction	WR	Cam.	31	12	62	14C3	25

Station or line	Ownership at Closure	Pre-Group Company	Date Closed	Map Ref	Note
Moat Lane Junction	WR	Cam.	31 12 62	14C3	
Mochdre & Pabo	LMS	LNW	5 1 31	19D4	16
Moffat—Beattock	ScR	Cal.	6 12 54	30G3	29
Moira (Woodville Jn)— **Burton-on-Trent** (Swadlincote Jn) via Swadlincote	LMS	Mid.	4 10 47	16E5	17
Moira (East Jn)—**Nuneaton** (Ashby Jn)	LMS	LNW&Mid	13 4 31	16E5	
Mollington	LMR	BJ	7 3 60	20D4	
Molyneux Brow	LMS	LY	29 6 31	45B2	
Moniave—Dumfries (Cairn Valley Jn)	LMS	GSW	3 5 43	26A5	18
Monk Bretton	LMS	Mid.	27 9 37	42E2	
Monk Fryston	NER	NE	14 9 59	21D4	
Monks Lane Halt	SRy	LBSC	11 9 39	5C4	
Monkton	LMS	GSW	28 10 40	29E3	
Monkton & Came Halt	SR	GW	7 1 57	3F3	
Monmouth (Troy)— Chepstow (Wye Valley Jn)	WR	GW	5 1 59	8A2	19
Monmouth (Troy)— Pontypool Road (Little Mill Jn)	WR	GW	13 6 55	8A2	20
Monmouth (Troy)— Ross-on-Wye	WR	GW	5 1 59	9E1	21
Monsal Dale	LMR	Mid.	10 8 59	15B5	
Montgreenan	ScR	GSW	7 3 55	29D3	
Montrose—Dubton Junction (Broomfield Jn)	LMS	Cal.	30 4 34	34C2	
Montrose—Dubton Junction	ScR	NB/Cal.	4 8 52	34C2	30
Monument Lane	LMR	LNW	17 11 58	13C3	
Moore	LMS	LNW	1 2 43	45D4	
Moorgate Halt	LMR	—	2 5 55	21F1✠	
Moor Row (Cleator Moor Jn)— **Siddick**	LMS	CWJ	13 4 31	26F3	23
Moretonhampstead—Newton Abbot	WR	GW	2 3 59	2B4	28
Moreton-on-Lugg	WR	S&H	9 6 58	9C1	
Morley (Top)	NER	GN	2 1 61	42B3	
Morpeth—Reedsmouth	NER	NB	15 9 52	27A5	24
Moss	NER	NE	8 6 53	21E5	
Mossend	ScR	Cal.	5 11 62	44B3	
Moss Halt—Wrexham (Moss Valley Jn)	GW	GW	1 1 31	20E4	*
Moss Side	LMR	PWY	26 6 61	24D4	
Mosstowie	ScR	HR	7 3 55	36C2	
Mount Melville	LNE	NB	22 9 30	34F4	
Mount Pleasant Road Halt	SRy	LSW	2 1 28	2B3✠	
Mount Vernon	LMS	Cal.	16 8 43	44C3	
Muir Of Ord	ScR	HR	13 6 60	35D5	
Mumbles Pier—Swansea (Rutland Street): **Mumbles Pier—Southend**	SWT	Mum.	12 10 59	43G3	*

Station or line	Ownership at Closure	Pre-Group Company	Date Closed			Map Ref	Note
Southend—Swansea (Rutland Street)	SWT	Mum.	5	1	60	43G3	*
Murrow (West)	ER	GN&GE	6	7	53	17F3	
Murtle	LNE	GNS	5	4	37	37G4	
Musgrave	LMR	NE	3	11	52	27F2	
Mutley	GW	GW	2	7	39	1A2	

1. Macduff—Turriff* 1.8.61. **2.** *Caerphilly* (East Branch Jn—West Branch Jn) remains open on main line. **3.** *2.5.60. **4.** Maldon West—Woodham Ferrers* 1.4.53; Maldon East—Maldon West* 31.1.59. **5.** Cl. 12.2.51, RO 2.4.51 *12.11.62. **6.** Glapwell—Pleasley West Jnø. **7.** *20.12.26. New line 1m. 48ch. opened from a point 2m. 52ch. from Broadstairs to a point 3m. 74ch. from Minster. New stations opened at Dumpton Park (11.7.26) and Ramsgate. Margate (West) RN Margate 11.7.26. **8.** Saxondale Jn—Barnstone Cement Sidings* 10.9.62. Workmen's service operated from Market Harborough—East Norton until 20.5.57. Marefield Jn—Welham Jn* 4.11.63; Marefield Jn—Melton Mowbray (North)* 1.6.64. **9.** Trains diverted to MSW line but Marlborough stn. retained for freight. **10.** RO 12.7.43 (Bomb damage). **11.** *11.11.63. **14.** Chadderton Jn—Oldham (Werneth)*. **15.** Fordham remains open on Ely—Newmarket Line. **16.** Cl. 1.1.17, RO 5.5.19. **17.** Woodville —Woodville Jn* 8.12.62; Swadlincote Jn (Cadley Hill Siding)—Woodville Jn (Church Gresley Colliery) *2.3.64. **18.** *4.7.49. **19.** Monmouth (Troy)—Tintern* 6.1.64. **20.** Monmouth (Troy)—Usk*. Closed by ASLEF strike on 28.5.55. Usk—Pontypool Road* 13.10.57. Workmen's service ran to Glascoed ROF until 13.10.57. **21.** Monmouth (May Hill)— Lydbrook Jn*; Monmouth (Troy—May Hill)* –.10.63. **22.** Merthyr Vale—Quakers Yard (H.L.)*. **23.** Cleator Moor Jn—Distington Jt. Jn* 1.7.63. **24.** Reedsmouth—Woodburn* 11.11.63. **25.** Llanidloes—Talyllyn Jn*; but Builth Road (LL) Goods Yard still served via Spur. **26.** Line at Tooting Jn severed and buffer stops erected. **27.** West Wemyss—Thornton Jn (East Jn)* 2.12.63. **28.** Moretonhampstead—Bovey* 6.4.64. **29.** *6.4.64. **30.** Broomfield Jn—Dubton Jn* –.7.63. **31.** *14.8.60. **32.** Retained after branch closed for Summer Saturday trains, as a relief to Weymouth. **33.** Trains diverted to ex LBSC stn. **34.** *4.5.64.

Station or line	Ownership at Closure	Pre-Group Company	Date Closed			Map Ref	Note
Naburn	NER	NE	8	6	53	21C5	
Nailsworth—Stonehouse (Bristol Road)	LMR	Mid.	8	6	49	9F3	1
Nantlle—Penygroes	LMS	LNW	8	8	32	19E2	2
Nantwich (Market Drayton Jn)—**Wellington** (Market Drayton Jn)	LMR	GW	9	9	63	15C2	
Nantybwch—Risca	WR	LNW	13	6	60	43C1	3
Nantyderry	WR	GW	9	6	58	43A2	
Nantymoel—Tondu	WR	GW	5	5	58	43D3	
Napsbury	LMR	Mid.	14	9	59	11G1	
Nassington	ER	LNW	1	7	57	17F1	
Navenby	ER	GN	10	9	62	16B1	
Naworth	NER	NE	5	5	52	27C1	
Nelson—Pontypridd (Pont-shon-Norton Jn)	GW	TV	'_	9	32	43C3	15

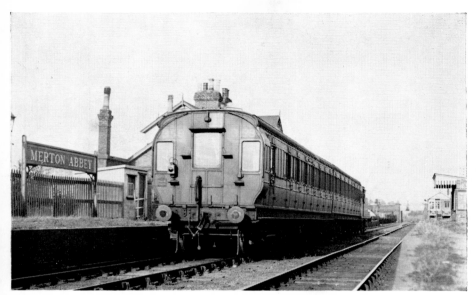

ABOVE: *The Tooting branch push-pull train pauses at Merton Abbey on August 23, 1927.*
[H. C. CASSERLEY

BELOW: *L.M.S. Sentinel steam rail car at Strathpeffer in May 1928.* [H. C. CASSERLEY

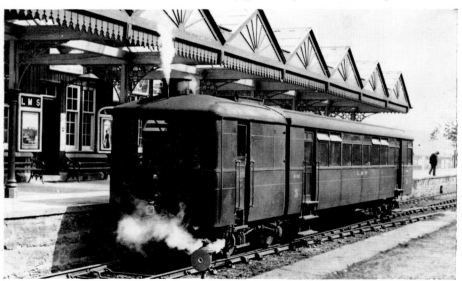

ABOVE: *A diesel multiple-unit forming the 2.28 p.m. from Northampton Castle to Bedford arrives at Piddington on March 4, 1961.* [G. DANIELS

BELOW: *Class L1 2-6-4T No. 67723 at West Green with the 4.50 p.m. North Woolwich to Palace Gates on April 26, 1962.* [L. A. DENCH

Station or line	Ownership at Closure	Pre-Group Company	Date Closed			Map Ref	Note
Nethercleugh	ScR	Cal.	13	6	60	26A3	
Newburgh (Glenburnie Jn)—							
St. Fort	ScR	NB	12	2	51	34F5	4
Newburn	NER	NE	15	9	58	27B5	
Newbury (Enborne Jn)—							
Shawford (Shawford Jn)	SR	GW/LSW	7	3	60	4A3	13
Newbury (West Fields) Halt	WR	GW	4	2	57	4A3	
Newby Bridge	LMR	Fur.	12	7	49	24A4✠	5
Newby Wiske	LNE	NE	2	9	46	21A3	
Newcastle (Brampton) Halt	LMS	—	2	4	23	20F1✠	
Newcastle Emlyn—Pencader	WR	GW	15	9	52	13F3	
Newhailes	ScR	NB	6	2	50	30B2	
New Hall Bridge Halt	LMR	LY	27	9	48	24D1	
Newham	NER	NE	25	9	50	31E5	6
Newpark	ScR	Cal.	14	9	59	30C3	
Newport	SRy	FYN	1	8	23	4F3	
Newport—Sandown	SR	IWC	6	2	56	4F3	*
New Radnor—Leominster:							
New Radnor—Kington	WR	GW	5	2	51	14E2	7
Kington—Leominster	WR	GW	7	2	55	14E2	
New Romney—Lydd							
(Romney Jn)	SRy	SEC	4	7	37	6E3	14*
Newsholme	LMR	LY	6	8	57	24C1	
Newtonhill	ScR	Cal.	11	6	56	34A1	
Newton Road	LMS	LNW	7	5	45	13B3	
Nidd Bridge	NER	NE	18	6	62	21C3	
Nigg	ScR	HR	13	6	60	36B4	
Nightingale Valley Halt	GW	—	23	9	29	8C2✠	
Nine Mile Point	WR	LNW	2	2	59	43B3	
Nocton & Dunston	ER	GN&GE	2	5	55	17B1	
Northampton (St. John's)	LMS	Mid.	3	7	39	10B2	8*
North Drove	ER	MGN	15	9	58	17E2	
Northfield—Old Hill:							
Northfield (Halesowen Jn)—							
Halesowen	GW&Mid.	GW&Mid.	–	4	19	9A4	12
Halesowen—Old Hill	GW	GW	5	12	27	15G4	11
North Greenwich—Millwall							
Junction	LNE	GE	4	5	26	40D3	*
North Leith—Abbeyhill							
(London Road Jn)	LNE	NB	16	6	47	30F2	
Northolt	WR	GW	21	11	48	39B1	
Northorpe (Higher)	NER	LNW	5	10	53	42C4	
Northorpe (Lincs)	ER	GC	4	7	55	22G4	
North Rode	LMR	NS	7	5	62	15B3	
North Walsall	LMS	Mid.	13	7	25	15F4	
North Walsham (**Town Stn.—**							
Antingham Road Jn)	ER	MGN	30	9	57	18D2	9
Northwich (Sandbach Jn)—							
Sandbach	LMR	LNW	4	1	60	20D2	
Norton (Ches)	LMR	BJ	1	9	52	45D4	
Norton Fitzwarren	WR	GW	30	10	61	8F4	
Norton-on-Tees	NER	NE	7	3	60	28E5	

Station or line	Ownership at Closure	Pre-Group Company	Date Closed			Map Ref	Note
Norwich (City)—Melton Constable	ER	MGN	2	3	59	18F3	10
Norwich (Trowse)	LNE	GE	5	9	39	18F3	
Nottingham **(London Road LL —Trent Lane West Jn)**	LNE	GN	22	5	44	41G5	
Nunburnholme	NER	NE	1	4	51	22C5	
Nursling	SR	LSW	16	9	57	4D4	

1. PC. TC 16.6.47. **2.** Cl. 1.1.17 RO 5.5.19. *2.12.63. **3.** Nantybwch—Sirhowy*. Nine Mile Point (q.v.) to Risca was GW. Sirhowy—Tredegar* 4.11.63. **4.** Glenburnie Jn— Lindores* 17.4.60. **5.** PC. TC 12.9.39. **6.** Cl. 5.5.41, RO 7.10.46. **7.** New Radnor— Dolyhir* 31.12.51; Dolyhir—Kington* 9.6.58. **8.** Connection with main line reversed and trains diverted to Northampton (Castle). **9.** *5.5.58. New spur then opened from North Walsham (Main) southwards to MGN line and used only by 'Holiday Camps Express' during summer of 1958. *2.3.59. **10.** Melton Constable—Themelthorpe* 12.9.60, upon opening of new spur from Whitwell & Reepham to Reepham (GE). **11.** Workmen's service continued and withdrawn 1.9.58. **12.** Workmen's service continued and withdrawn 4.1.60. Halesowen—Rubery* 6.1.64. **13.** Cl. (P) 4.8.42, RO 8.3.43. Trains on summer Saturdays continued to run from Shawford Jn to Winchester (Chesil) until 11.9.61. **14.** New line, 3m 65ch., opened from a point 45 chains from New Romney to a point on Dungeness branch 2m. 10ch. from Lydd, known as Lydd Jn. Lydd renamed Lydd Town; new stations opened at Lydd-on-Sea and Greatstone-on-Sea. **15.** Albion Colliery—Llancaiach*.

Station or line	Ownership at Closure	Pre-Group Company	Date Closed			Map Ref	Note
Oakdale	GW	—	12	9	32	43B2✠	
Oakley	LMR	Mid.	15	9	58	10B1	
Oakley	SR	LSW	17	6	63	4B3	
Oddington Halt	LMS	LNW	25	10	26	10E4	
Offord & Buckden	ER	GN	2	2	59	11C2	
Old Colwyn	LMR	LNW	1	12	52	19D4	
Old Dalby	LMR	Mid.	4	2	57	16D3	
Oldham (Clegg Street)	LMR	OAGB	4	5	59	21D1	
Old Leake	ER	GN	17	9	56	17C3	
Old Meldrum—Inverurie	LNE	GNS	2	11	31	37E3	
Old Oak Lane Halt	GW	GW	30	6	47	39C3	
Oldwoods Halt	WR	GW	12	9	60	20G3	
Old Ynysybwl Halt— Pontypridd (Clydach Court Jn)	WR	TV	28	7	52	43C3	6
Onibury	WR	S&H	9	6	58	14C1	
Ordsall Lane	LMR	LNW	4	2	57	45B3	
Ormside	LMR	Mid.	2	6	52	27E2	
Ormskirk—Rainford Jn	LMR	LY	5	11	56	45E2	1
Orton Waterville	LMS	LNW	5	10	42	17F1	
Orwell	ER	GE	15	6	59	12D3	
Osmondthorpe Halt	NER	NE	7	3	60	42A2✠	
Oswestry	GW	GW	7	7	24	20G4	5

Station or line	Ownership at Closure	Pre-Group Company	Date Closed			Map Ref	Note
Otterington	NER	NE	15	9	58	21A4	
Otterspool	LMR	CLC	5	3	51	45F4	
Oughty Bridge	ER	GC	15	6	59	42F2	
Over & Wharton— Hartford (Winsford Jn)	LMS	LNW	16	6	47	20D2	2
Overtown	LMS	Cal.	5	10	42	30D5	
Oxenhope—Keighley	NER	Mid.	1	1	62	21D1	3
Oxford (Kennington Jn)— **Princes Risborough**	WR	GW	7	1	63	10E4	
Oxford (Rewley Road)	WR	LNW	1	10	51	10E4	4
Oxford Road Halt	LMS	LNW	25	10	26	10E4	
Oxheys	LMS	LNW	28	2	25	24D3	

1. Ormskirk—Skelmersdale* 4.11.63.   **2.** *18.3.49.   **3.** Oxenhope—Ingrow GN Jn* 18.6.62.
4. Trains diverted to Oxford (General) (GW).   **5.** Trains diverted to ex. Cam. station.
6. Old Ynysybwl Halt—Ynysybwl, Windsor Passing Sdg—Clydach Court Jn*; Ynysybwl—
Lady Windsor Colliery* 2.11.59.

Station or line	Ownership at Closure	Pre-Group Company	Date Closed			Map Ref	Note
Padeswood & Buckley	LMR	LNW	6	1	58	20E5	
Padgate—Sankey (direct)	LMR	CLC	9	9	63	45C4	
Palace Gates—Seven Sisters	ER	GE	7	1	63	40A5	
Palnure	ScR	PPW	7	5	51	25B4	
Pandy	WR	GW	9	6	58	14G1	
Panteg & Griffithstown (Coed-y-Gric Jn)—**Pontypool Road**	WR	GW	30	4	62	43A2	
Pant Glas	LMR	LNW	7	1	57	19E2	
Parcyrhun Halt	WR	—	13	6	55	43G1✠	
Park Drain	ER	GN&GE	7	2	55	22F5	
Parkeston Quay (West)— Parkeston Quay	ER	—	11	5	60	12E3✠	
Parkgate & Aldwarke	ER	GC	29	10	51	42F1	
Parkhead (North)	ScR	NB	19	9	55	44D3	
Parkhill	ScR	GNS	3	4	50	37F4	
Park Royal	GW	GW	26	9	37	39C3	
Park Royal West Halt	GW	GW	30	6	47	39C3✠	
Pateley Bridge—Harrogate (Ripley Valley Jn)	NER	NE	2	4	51	21B2	
Paulsgrove Halt	SRy	—	28	6	33	4E2✠	
Peakirk	ER	GN	11	9	61	17F2	
Peebles—Symington	ScR	Cal.	5	6	50	30D2	1
Pelton	NER	NE	7	12	53	27C5	
Penarth Dock	WR	TV	1	1	62	43B5	
Pendlebury	LMR	LY	3	10	60	45B2	
Penicuik—Rosewell & Hawthornden	ScR	NB	10	9	51	30	

Station or line	Ownership at Closure	Pre-Group Company	Date Closed			Map Ref	Note
Penpergwm	WR	GW	9	6	58	43A1	
Penygraig—Llantrisant	WR	GW	9	6	58	43D3	
Perivale Halt	GW	GW	30	6	47	39C2	
Persley Halt	LNE	GNS	5	4	37	37F4	
Petersfield—Pulborough:							
Petersfield—Midhurst	SR	LSW	7	2	55	4D2	*
Midhurst—Pulborough							
(Hardham Jn)	SR	LBSC	7	2	55	4D1	
Philpstoun	ScR	NB	18	6	51	30B3	
Pickering—Pilmoor							
(South Jn)	NER	NE	2	2	53	22A5	3
Pickering—Seamer	NER	NE	5	6	50	22A5	4
Pickhill	NER	NE	14	9	59	21A3	
Picton	NER	NE	4	1	60	28F5	
Piel—Barrow (Salthouse Jn)	LMS	Fur.	6	7	36	24B4	*
Pilmoor	NER	NE	5	5	58	21B4	
Pilsley	LMR	GC	2	11	59	41D3	
Pinchbeck	ER	GN&GE	11	9	61	17E2	
Pinchingthorpe	NER	NE	29	10	51	28E4	
Pinxton (South)—Kimberley							
(East) (Awsworth Jn)	LMR	GN	7	1	63	41E3	5
Pitfodels Halt	LNE	GNS	5	4	37	37G4	
Pitsford & Brampton	LMR	LNW	5	6	50	10B2	
Plaidy	LNE	GNS	22	5	44	37D3	
Plains	ScR	NB	18	6	51	44A4	
Plas-y-court Halt	WR	—	12	9	60	14A2✠	
Platt Bridge	LMR	LNW	1	5	61	45D2	
Plawsworth	NER	NE	7	4	52	27C5	
Plean	ScR	Cal.	11	6	56	30A5	
Pleasley (Pleasley West Jn)—							
Westhouses & Blackwell	LMS	Mid.	28	7	30	41D4	
Pleck	LMR	LNW	17	11	58	13A2✠	
Plessey Halt	NER	NE	15	9	58	27B5	
Plumpton	LMR	LNW	31	5	48	27D1	
Plumtree	LMR	Mid.	28	2	49	16D3	
Plymouth (Millbay)—							
Plymouth (North Road)	GW	GW	23	4	41	1D5	
Plymouth (Friary)—							
Plymouth (North Road)							
(Lipson Jn)	WR	LSW	15	9	58	1D5	
Plympton	WR	GW	2	3	59	2D5	
Polton—Eskbank (Esk							
Valley Jn)	ScR	NB	10	9	51	30C2	12
Pont Lliw	GW	GW	22	9	24	43G2	
Ponthir	WR	GW	30	4	62	43A3	
Pont Lawrence Halt	WR	LNW	4	2	57	43B3	
Pontrilas	WR	GW	9	6	58	14G1	
Pontyrhyll—Port Talbot							
(Central):							
Pontyrhyll—Maesteg							
(Neath Road)	GW	PT	12	9	32	43D3	6

Station or line	Ownership at Closure	Pre-Group Company	Date Closed	Map Ref	Note
Maesteg (Neath Road)— **Port Talbot (Central)**	GW	PT	11 9 33	43E3	13
Poplar—Dalston Junction	LMS	NL	15 5 44	40C3	11
Portbury	WR	GW	30 4 62	8C2	
Portbury Shipyard	GW	—	26 3 23	8C2✠	
Port Carlisle—Drumburgh	LNE	NB	1 6 32	26C2	*
Port Clarence— **Billingham-on-Tees:** **Port Clarence—Haverton Hill**	LNE	NE	11 9 39	28E4	
Haverton Hill— **Billingham-on-Tees**	NER	NE	6 11 61	28E4	
Port Dinorwic	LMR	LNW	12 9 60	19D2	
Porthcawl—Pyle	WR	GW	9 9 63	43E4	
Portishead—Weston-Super- **Mare**	WCP	WCP	20 5 40	8C2	*
Portishead	WR	GW	4 1 54	8C2	7
Portlethen	ScR	Cal.	11 6 56	37G4	
Port Meadow Halt	LMS	LNW	25 10 26	10E4	
Portpatrick—Stranraer **(Town)**	ScR	PPW	6 2 50	25C1	8
Portsmouth (Lancs)	LMR	LY	7 7 58	20A1	
Port Victoria—Gravesend **(Central):** **Port Victoria—Grain** **Crossing Halt**	SR	SEC	11 6 51	6B4	*
Grain—Gravesend (Central) (Hoo Jn)	SR	SEC	4 12 61	6B4	9
Postland	ER	GN&GE	11 9 61	17E2	
Potterhanworth	ER	GN&GE	2 5 55	17B1	
Poulton Curve Halt	LMR	PWY	1 12 52	24D4	
Presteign—Titley	WR	GW	4 6 51	14D2	10
Preston Brook	LMR	LNW	1 3 48	20C3	
Priestfield—Stourbridge Jn	WR	GW	30 7 62	15G3	
Princetown—Yelverton	WR	GW	5 3 56	2C5	*
Probus & Ladock Platform	WR	GW	2 12 57	1E2	
Purfleet Rifle Range Halt	LMR	Mid.	31 5 48	5B5✠	
Pye Bridge **(Ironville Jn—** **Codnore Park Jn)**	LMS	Mid.	16 6 47	41E3	
Pyle—Tondu	WR	GW	9 9 63	43E4	
Pyle **(West Jn—Heol-y-Sheet** **Crossing)**	WR	—	9 9 63	43E4✠	

1. Peebles (Cal.)—Broughton* 7.6.54. Peebles (West) (Cal.)—Peebles (NB)* 1.8.59. **3.** Pickering—Kirby Moorside*. **4.** Thornton Dale—Seamer*; Pickering—Thornton Dale* -.11.62. **5.** Pinxton South—Eastwood & Langley Mill*. **6.** Pontyrhyll—Llety Bronguø; Llety Brongu—Cwmduø; **7.** Station closed and new one opened 20 chains nearer Bristol. **8.** Portpatrick—Colfin*; Colfin—Stranraer (Town)* 1.4.59. **9.** New station at Grain opened immediately east of Grain Crossing Halt on 3.9.51. when latter closed. **10.** PC. TC 5.2.51. **11.** Substitute bus service provided until 23.4.45. **12.** *4.5.64. **13.** Tonygroes Jn—Port Talbot (Central) *2.2.60; Duffryn Jn—Tonygroes Jn *27.3.63.

Station or line	Ownership at Closure	Pre-Group Company	Date Closed	Map Ref	Note
Quainton Road	LMR	MGC	4 3 63	10E3	
Quainton Road—Verney Junction	MGC	MGC	6 7 36	10D3	*
Queenborough Pier— Queenborough	SRy	SEC	1 3 23	6B4	1
Quorn & Woodhouse	LMR	GC	4 3 63	16E4	

1. Cl. –.10.14 RO 27.12.22,* –.–.39.

Station or line	Ownership at Closure	Pre-Group Company	Date Closed	Map Ref	Note
Radcliffe Bridge	LMR	LY	7 7 58	45B2	
Rainford Junction—Widnes	LMR	LNW	18 6 51	45E2	14
Ramsey (East)—Somersham	LNE	GN&GE	22 9 30	11B2	1
Ramsey (North)—Holme	LNE	GN	6 10 47	11A2	
Ramsgate (Harbour)— Broadstairs	SRy	SEC	2 7 26	6B1	*11
Ramsgate (Town)— Minster	SRy	SEC	2 7 26	6B1	*11
Ranskill	ER	GN	6 10 58	16A3	
Raskelf	NER	NE	5 5 58	21B4	
Ratho	ScR	NB	18 6 51	30B3	
Ratho (Low Level)	LNE	NB	22 9 30	30B3	
Ravelrig—Slateford (Balerno Jn) via Balerno	LMS	Cal.	1 11 43	30C3	
Ravenscraig	LMS	Cal.	1 2 44	29B3	
Ravensthorpe (Lower)	NER	LY	30 6 52	42C4	
Rearsby	LMR	Mid.	2 4 51	16E3	
Redmarshall	NER	NE	31 3 52	28E5	2
Rednal & West Felton	WR	GW	12 9 60	20G4	
Red Rock	LMR	LUJ	26 9 49	45D2	
Red Wharf Bay—Holland Arms	LMS	LNW	22 9 30	19D2	*
Reedley Hallows Halt	LMR	LY	3 12 56	24D1	
Renfrew (Porterfield)— Cardonald	LMS	G&P	19 7 26	44F4	13
Renishaw (Central)	ER	GC	4 3 63	41B3	
Reston—St. Boswells: Reston—Duns	ScR	NB	10 9 51	31C3	
Duns—St. Boswells (Ravenswood Jn)	ScR	NB	12 8 48	31C2	3
Retford (Clarborough Jn)— Saxilby (Sykes Jn)	ER	GC	2 11 59	16A2	*
Rhiwderin	WR	BM	28 2 54	43A3	
Rhos—Wrexham (Rhos Jn)	GW	GW	1 1 31	20E4	4
Rhosymedre Halt	WR	GW	2 3 59	20F4	
Rhu	ScR	NB	9 1 56	29B3	5

Station or line	Ownership at Closure	Pre-Group Company	Date Closed	Map Ref	Note
Rhydyfelin Halt— Coryton Halt	GW	Car.	20 7 31	43C3	*
Rhymney—Rhymney Bridge	WR	LNW&Rhy	21 9 53	43C1	12
Rhymney (Lower)—Pengam (Mon):					
Rhymney (Lower)—New Tredegar	GW	BM	14 4 30	43C2	*
New Tredegar—Pengam (Mon) (Aberbargoed Jn)	WR	BM	31 12 62	43B2	*6
Riby Street Platform	LNE	—	14 4 41	22F2✠	
Riccall	NER	NE	15 9 58	21D5	
Richborough Castle Halt	SRy	—	11 9 39	6C2✠	
Rickmansworth (Church Street)—Watford (Croxley Green Jn)	LMR	LNW	3 3 52	5A2	
Rickmansworth **(Watford North Jn—Watford East Jn)**	LTE	—	4 1 60	5A2✠	7
Rigg	LMS	GSW	1 11 40	26B2	
Rillington	LNE	NE	22 9 30	22B5	
Rimington	LMR	LY	7 7 58	24C1	
Ringley Road	LMR	LY	5 1 53	45B2	
Ripley—Derby (Little Eaton Jn)	LMS	Mid.	1 6 30	41F2	8
Rishworth—Sowerby Bridge	LMS	LY	8 7 29	21E1	9
Robins Lane Halt	LMS	—	26 9 38	45D3✠	
Robroyston	ScR	Cal.	11 6 56	44D4	
Roffey Road Halt	SRy	LBSC	3 1 37	5E2	
Rogart	ScR	HR	13 6 60	36A5	
Rolleston-on-Dove	LMR	NS	1 1 49	15D5	
Rosherville Halt	SRy	SEC	16 7 33	5B5	
Rossington	ER	GN	6 10 58	21F5	
Rothbury—Scotsgap	NER	NB	15 9 52	31G4	14
Rotherham Road	ER	GC	5 1 53	42F1	
Rotherham (Westgate)— Holmes	ER	Mid.	6 10 52	42F1	
Rothley	LMR	GC	4 3 63	16E4	
Royston & Notton (Royston Jn)**—Thornhill** (Midland Jn)	NER	Mid.	13 6 60	42D2	
Ruddington	LMR	GC	4 3 63	41G5	
Rumworth & Daubhill	LMR	LNW	3 3 52	45C2	
Rushcliffe Halt	LMR	GC	4 3 63	16D4	
Ruskington	ER	GN&GE	11 9 61	17C1	
Rutherglen **(Clyde Bridge Jn— Rutherglen W. Jn)**	ScR	Cal.	13 6 60	44D3	
Ruthrieston	LNE	GNS	5 4 37	37G4	
Ryhope (East)	NER	NE	7 3 60	28C5	
Ryton	NER	NE	5 7 54	27D5	

1. Ramsey (East)—Warboys* 20.8.57. **2.** Formerly Carlton RN 1.10.23. **3.** Duns—Greenlaw* due to floods. **4.** *14.10.63. **5.** Formerly Row, and RO as a halt 4.4.60. **6.** Elliott Colliery is still worked, from Brithdir (Rhy). **7.** Freight service withdrawn 6.3.60, but still used for ECS workings. **8.** Ripley—Marehay Crossing* 1.4.63. **9.** Rishworth—Ripponden* –.2.53; Ripponden—Sowerby Bridge* 1.9.58. **10.** *St. Helens* (Gerard's Bridge Jn—Sutton

R-S

Oak Jn) remains open on Liverpool—Manchester line. **11.** New line 1m. 48ch. opened from a point 2m. 52ch. from Broadstairs to a point 3m. 74ch. from Minster. New station opened at Dumpton Park (11.7.26) and Ramsgate. **12.** *-.-.55. **13.** Kings Inch—Deansideø. **14.** *11.11.63.

Station or line	Ownership at Closure	Pre-Group Company	Date Closed	Map Ref	Note
St. Albans (Abbey)— **Hatfield**	LMR/ER	GN	1 10 51	11F2	
St. Anthony's	NER	NE	12 9 60	28B5✠	
St. Annes Road	THJ	THJ	9 8 42	40A4	
St. Blazey	GW	GW	21 9 25	1D3	
St. Devereux	WR	GW	9 6 58	14F1	
St. Dunstan's	NER	GN	15 9 52	42A4	
St. Helens (Central)— **Lowton St. Mary's**	LMR	GC	3 3 52	45D3	
St. James Deeping	ER	GN	11 9 61	17F2	
St. Lawrence	SRy	SEC	2 7 26	6B1	
St. Mary's	LPTB	MD	1 5 38	40C4	
St. Quintin Park & Wormwood Scrubs	WL	WL	3 10 40	39C4	
St. Rollox	ScR	Cal.	5 11 62	44D4	
Salisbury	GW	GW	12 9 32	4C5	
Saltney	WR	GW	12 9 60	20D4	
Salwick	LMS	PWY	2 5 38	24D3	
Sandal	NER	WRG	4 11 57	42C2	
Sandgate—Sandling Jn: **Sandgate—Hythe (Kent)**	SRy	SEC	1 4 31	6D2	*
Hythe (Kent)—Sandling Jn	SR	SEC	3 12 51	6D3	*5
Sandon	LMS	NS	6 1 47	15D4	
Sandwich Road—Eastry	EK	EK	1 11 28	6C2	1
Sandycroft	LMR	LNW	1 5 61	20D4	
Sankey Bridges	LMR	LNW	26 9 49	45D4	2
Sauchie	LNE	NB	22 9 30	30A4	
Saughall	LMR	GC	1 2 54	20D4	
Saughton	NB	NB	1 3 21	30B3	
Saughtree	LNE	NE	1 12 44	31G1	3
Sawley	LMS	Mid.	1 12 30	16D4	
Saxby	LMR	Mid.	6 2 61	16E2	
Saxby—Sutton Bridge: **Saxby—Sutton Bridge** (via Spalding)	LMR/ER	Mid/MGN	2 3 59	16E2	19
Spalding **(Cuckoo Junction— Welland Bank Jn)**	ER	MGN	15 9 58	17E2	20
Scafell Halt	WR	Cam.	7 3 55	14C3	
Scalby	NER	NE	2 3 53	22A4	
Schoolhill	LNE	GNS	5 4 37	37G4	
Scopwick & Timberland	ER	GN&GE	7 11 55	17C1	
Scorton	LMS	LNW	1 5 39	24C3	
Scotby	LMS	Mid.	1 2 42	26C1	
Scotby	NER	NE	2 11 59	26C1	
Scotch Dyke	ScR	NB	2 5 49	26B1	

ABOVE: *L.M.S. 0-4-4T No. 41900 stands at Upton-on-Severn with the branch train to Ashchurch on August 23, 1958.* [E. WILMSHURST

BELOW: *Class L1 2-6-4T No. 67764 with the 12.27 p.m. from Middlesbrough to Scarborough at Whitby West Cliff on May 1, 1958.* [L. A. DENCH

ABOVE: *Wantage Tramway 0-4-0T No. 5 nears Wantage with a freight train on May 10, 1930.*
[H. C. CASSERLEY

BELOW: *G.W. 0-6-0 No. 3210 waits at Wallingford with the branch train to Cholsey & Moulsford on June 7, 1958.*
[G. DANIELS

Station or line	Ownership at Closure	Pre-Group Company	Date Closed	Map Ref	Note
Scremerston	NER	NE	8 7 51	31D4	
Scrooby	LNE	GN	14 9 31	21G5	
Seacombe & Egremont—					
Bidston (Seacombe Jn)	LMR	Wir.	4 1 60	45F3	
Seacroft	ER	GN	7 12 53	17B4	
Seahouses—Chathill	NSL	NSL	29 10 51	31E5	*
Seaton—Workington (Calva Jn)	CWJ	CWJ	– 2 22	26E3	
Seaton	NER	NE	1 9 52	28C5	
Sedbergh	LMR	LNW	1 2 54	27G2	
Sedgebrook	ER	GN	2 7 56	16D2	
Seedley	LMR	LNW	2 1 56	45B3	
Sefton Park	LMR	LNW	2 5 60	45F4	
Selsdon—Woodside	CO	CO	1 1 17	5C3	22
Selsey—Chichester	ST	ST	19 1 35	4F1	*
Selkirk—Galashiels	ScR	NB	10 9 51	30E1	
Sellafield—Whitehaven (Mire House Jn)	LMS	WCE	16 6 47	26F3	18
Sessay	NER	NE	15 9 58	21B4	
Seton Mains Halt	LNE	NB	22 9 30	30B1✠	
Seven Sisters—South Tottenham	ER	GE	7 1 63	40A4	
Shadwell & St. Georges East	LNE	GE	7 7 41	40C4	
Sharlston	NER	LY	3 3 58	42C1	
Sharnbrook	LMR	Mid.	2 5 60	10B1	
Sheerness Dockyard	SEC	SEC	2 1 22	6B4	24
Shields Road (**Shields Road Jn—Larkfield Jn**)	ScR	Cal.	13 6 60	44F1	
Shilton	LMR	LNW	16 9 57	16G5	
Shipley (Bridge Street)— Laisterdyke	LNE	GN	2 2 31	42A4	
Shipley Gate	LMR	Mid.	27 8 48	41F3	
Shipston-on-Stour— Moreton-in-Marsh	GW	GW	8 7 29	9C5	4
Shoreditch	LMS	NL	4 10 40	40C4	
Shoreham Airport (Bungalow Town) Halt	SRy	SRy	15 7 40	5F2	6
Shotley Bridge	NER	NE	21 9 53	27C4	
Shrewsbury (Abbey)— Llanymynech	S&M	S&M	6 11 33	15E1	7
Sibsey	ER	GN	11 9 61	17C3	
Sideway Halt	LMS	—	2 4 23	15C3✠	
Silverdale (Crown Street) Halt	LMR	NS	7 6 49	20F1✠	
Sinderby	NER	NE	1 1 62	21A3	
Skinningrove	NER	NE	30 6 52	28E3	
Skirlaugh	NER	NE	6 5 57	22D3	
Smeafield	LNE	NE	1 5 30	31D4	
Smeaton	LNE	NB	22 9 30	30C1	
Smeeth	SR	SEC	4 1 54	6D3	
Smithy Bridge	LMR	LY	2 5 60	45A1	
Snailham Halt	SR	SEC	2 2 59	6E4✠	
Snatchwood Halt	WR	GW	5 10 53	43A2	

Station or line	Ownership at Closure	Pre-Group Company	Date Closed			Map Ref	Note
Soho	LMR	LNW	23	5	49	13C2	
Soho Road	LMS	LNW	5	5	41	13B3	
Somerset Road	LMS	Mid.	28	7	30	15G4	
Somerton	WR	GW	10	9	62	8F2	
South Acton—Acton Town	LTE	MD	2	3	59	39D3	*
Southburn	NER	NE	20	9	54	22C4	
Southerndown Road	WR	BRY	23	10	61	43D4	
South Harefield Halt	GW&GC	—	1	10	31	5A2✠	
Southport (Lord Street)— Gateacre:							
Southport (Lord Street)— Aintree (Central)	LMR	CLC	7	1	52	45F1	14
Aintree (Central)—Gateacre	LMR	CLC	7	11	60	45F3	
South Queensferry Halt— Dalmeny	LNE	NB	14	1	29	30B3	
South Shields (Westoe Lane) —Whitburn Colliery	SSM	SSM	20	11	53	28B5	
Southwaite	LMR	LNW	7	4	52	26D1	
Southwick	LMS	GSW	25	9	39	26C4	
Speke	LMS	LNW	22	9	30	45E4	
Spetisbury Halt	SR	SD	17	9	56	3E4	
Spilsby—Firsby	LNE	GN	10	9	39	17B3	9
Spratton	LMR	LNW	23	5	49	10A2	
Spring Vale	LMR	LY	5	8	58	20A2	
Sprouston	ScR	NE	4	7	55	31E2	
Stafford—Uttoxeter (Bromshall Jn)	LNE	GN	4	12	39	15D4	10
Staincliffe & Batley Carr	NER	LNW	7	4	52	42C3	
Staincross	LNE	GC	22	9	30	42D2	
Stainland—Greetland	LMS	LY	23	9	29	42C5	11
Stairfoot	ER	GC	16	9	57	42E2	
Stamford—Wansford	LNE	GN	1	7	29	17F1	*
Stamford (East)	ER	GN	4	3	57	17F1	12
Standish	LMR	LNW	23	5	49	45D1	
Standon Bridge	LMR	LNW	4	2	52	15D3	
Stanley	ScR	Cal.	11	6	56	33E5	
Stanmore (Village)—Belmont	LMR	LNW	15	9	52	5A2	
Stannington	NER	NE	15	9	58	27A5	
Stansfield Hall	LMR	LY	17	8	49	21E1	13
Stanwardine Halt	WR	—	12	9	60	20G4✠	
Staveley (Central)	ER	GC	4	3	63	41B3	
Staveley (Town)	ER	Mid.	5	8	52	41B3	
Stepps	ScR	Cal.	5	11	62	44C4	
Stobcross	ScR	Cal.	3	8	59	44E4	
Stockton (Redmarshall East Jn)**—Wellfield**	LNE	NE	2	11	31	28E5	
Stoke Canon	WR	GW	13	6	60	2B3	
Stoke Ferry—Denver	LNE	GE	22	9	30	17F5	
Stonecross Halt	SRy	LBSC	7	7	35	5F5	
Stonehall & Lydden Halt	SR	SEC	5	4	54	6C2✠	
Stoneywood	LNE	GNS	5	4	37	37F4	

Station or line	Ownership at Closure	Pre-Group Compay	Date Closed	Map Ref	Note
Storeton (for Barnston)	LMR	GC	3 12 51	20C4	
Stourbridge Junction (Brettall Lane Jn)—**Wolverhampton** (Oxley Jn) via Wombourn	GW	—	31 10 32	15G3✠	
Stourpaine & Durweston Halt	SR	—	17 9 56	3E4✠	
Stow Bardolph	ER	GE	4 11 63	17F4	
Stow Park	ER	GN&GE	11 9 61	16A2	
Strapp Lane Halt	WR	—	5 6 50	3C3✠	15
Stratford LL. (Channelsea Jn)—**Victoria Park**	LNE	GE	2 11 42	40B3	
Stratford Market	ER	GE	6 5 57	40B2	
Strathbungo	ScR	GBK	28 5 62	44E3	
Strathord	LMS	Cal.	13 4 31	33E5	
Strathpeffer—Dingwall (Fodderty Jn)	LMS	HR	23 2 46	35D5	16
Stravithie	LNE	NB	22 9 30	34F3	
Strensall	LNE	NE	22 9 30	21B5	
Stretton & Clay Mills	LMR	NS	1 1 49	15C5	
Stretton (for Ashover)	LMR	Mid.	11 9 61	41D2	
Stroud (Cheapside)— Dudbridge	LMR	Mid.	8 6 49	9E3	21
Sturton	ER	GC	2 2 59	16A2	
Summer Lane	ER	GC	29 6 59	42E2	
Sunilaws	NER	NE	4 7 55	31D2	
Surfleet	ER	GN	11 9 61	17D2	
Sutton Bingham Halt	SR	LSW	31 12 62	3E2	
Sutton Coldfield (Town)	LMS	Mid.	1 1 25	15F5	
Sutton-in-Ashfield (General) —**Sutton Junction**	LMR	Mid.	26 9 49	41D4	17
Sutton Weaver	LMS	LNW	30 11 31	45D5	
Swainsthorpe	ER	GE	5 7 54	18F3	
Swalwell	NER	NE	2 11 53	28B3	
Swanley Junction	SRy	SEC	16 4 39	5B4	23
Swannington	LMR	Mid.	18 6 51	16E5	
Swansea (East Dock)— Neath (Riverside)	GW	GW	28 9 36	43F3	
Swansea (Riverside)—Jersey Marine (Neath Loop Jn)	GW	RSB	11 9 33	43F3	
Swindon (Town)—Swindon Junction (Rushey Platt Jn)	WR	MSW	11 9 61	9G5	
Swinton (Central)	ER	GC	15 9 58	42F1	
Swiss Cottage	LPTB	Met.	18 8 40	39B5	

1. Eastry—Richborough* 27.10.49. **2.** Cl. 1.1.17 RO 1.7.19. **3.** RO 23.8.48 then PC 15.10.56 with line. **4.** *2.5.60. **5.** Cl. 3.5.43, RO 1.10.45. **6.** Cl. 1.1.33 RO 1.7.35. Formerly Bungalow Town Halt. **7.** *29.2.60. Operated by War Department since 1941. **9.** *1.12.58. **10.** *5.3.51. **11.** *14.9.59. **12.** Trains diverted to Stamford (Town). **13.** PC. TC 31.7.44. **14.** Southport (Lord St.)—Altcar & Hillhouse*; Altcar & Hillhouse—Aintreeө. **15.** Cl. 6.10.41, RO 16.12.46. **16.** *26.3.51. **17.** Cl. 1.1.17, RO 9.7.23, Cl. 4.5.26, RO 20.9.26. Workmen's service operated until *1.10.51. **18.** Cl. 7.1.35, RO 6.5.46. **19.** Bourne—South Witham*. **20.** *2.3.59. **21.** PC. TC 16.6.47. **22.** RO 30.9.35 upon electrification. **23.** Resited. New station opened 21 chains west. **24.** Upon opening of direct Queensborough-Sheerness-on-Sea line.

T

Station or line	Ownership at Closure	Pre-Group Company	Date Closed	Map Ref	Note
Talley Road Halt	WR	VT	4 4 55	13G5	
Tallington	ER	GN	15 6 59	17F1	
Tamerton Foliot Halt	SR	LSW	10 9 62	1D5	
Tarbolton	LMS	GSW	4 1 43	29E4	
Tean Halt	LMR	NS	1 6 53	15D4	
Temple Hirst	NER	NE	6 3 61	21E5	
Temple Sowerby	LMR	NE	7 12 53	27E1	
Tempsford	ER	GN	5 11 56	11C2	
Teston Crossing Halt	SR	SEC	2 11 59	6C5✠	
Thaxted—Elsenham	ER	GE	15 9 52	11E4	1
The Dyke—Dyke Jn Halt	SRy	LBSC	1 1 39	5F3	*6
Thelwall	LMR	LNW	17 9 56	45C4	
The Mound	ScR	HR	13 6 60	36A4	
The Oaks	LMR	LY	6 11 50	45B1	
Thorington	ER	GE	4 11 57	12E4	
Thornbridge Halt	LMS	—	1 8 38	30B4✠	
Thornbury—Yate	LMS	Mid.	19 6 44	9F2	
Thornhill	NER	LY	1 1 62	42C3	
Thornilee	ScR	NB	6 11 50	30E1	
Thorney	ER	MGN	2 12 57	17F2	
Thorpe-on-the-Hill	ER	Mid.	7 2 55	16B1	
Three Counties	ER	GN	5 1 59	11E2	
Thurstaston	LMR	BJ	1 2 54	20C5	
Tibshelf (Town)	LMR	GC	4 3 63	41D3	
Tidal Basin	LNE	GE	15 8 43	40C2	
Tidworth—Ludgershall	SR	MSW	19 9 55	4B5	2
Tilbury (Marine)	LMS	Mid.	1 5 32	5B5✠	
Tinsley	ER	GC	29 10 51	42G2	
Tochineal	ScR	GNS	1 10 51	37C1	
Toddington	WR	GW	7 3 60	9D4	
Tollesbury Pier—Kelvedon:					
Tollesbury Pier—Tollesbury	GE	GE	18 7 21	12F5	3
Tollesbury—Kelvedon	ER	GE	7 5 51	12F5	3
Topcliffe	NER	NE	14 9 59	21A4	
Tovil	SRy	SEC	15 3 43	6C5	
Towneley	LMR	LY	4 8 52	24E1	
Tram Inn	WR	GW	9 6 58	14F1	
Treborth	LMR	LNW	2 3 59	19D2	
Trehowell Halt	WR	—	29 10 51	20F4✠	
Trentham Gardens—					
Trentham	LMS	NS	– 9 27	15D3	
Treowen Halt	WR	—	11 7 60	43B2✠	
Trumpers Crossing Halt	GW	GW	1 2 26	39D2	
Turnchapel—Plymouth					
(Friary)	WR	LSW	10 9 51	1A2	4
Turnhouse	LNE	NB	22 9 30	30B3	
Turton & Edgworth	LMR	LY	6 2 61	45B1	
Tuxford (North)	ER	GN	4 7 55	16B2	
Twickenham	SR	LSW	28 3 54	39E2	5
Twizell	NER	NE	4 7 55	31D3	
Twywell	LMR	Mid.	30 7 51	10A1	

1. *1.6.53.   **2.** Taken over by War Dept. 25.11.55.   **3.** Tollesbury Pier—Tiptree (Tudwick Road Sdg)* 29.10.51; Tiptree (Tudwick Road Sdg)—Kelvedon* 1.10.62.   **4.** Turnchapel—Plymstock* 2.10.61.   **5.** New station opened 250 yards nearer St. Margarets.   **6.** Cl. 1.1.17, RO 26.7.20; Dyke Jn RN Aldrington Halt upon closure of branch.

Station or line	Ownership at Closure	Pre-Group Company	Date Closed			Map Ref	Note
Uffington & Barnack	ER	Mid.	1	9	52	17F1	
Unstone	ER	Mid.	29	10	51	41B2	
Upper Batley	NER	GN	4	2	52	42B3	
Upper Broughton	LMR	Mid.	31	5	48	16D3	
Upperthorpe & Killamarsh	LNE	GC	7	7	30	41B3	
Uppingham—Seaton	LMR	LNW	13	6	60	16F2	1
Upwell—Wisbech	LNE	GE	2	1	28	17F4	
Upwey Wishing Well Halt	SR	GW	7	1	57	3F3	
Usworth	NER	NE	9	9	63	28C5	
Utterby Halt	ER	GN	11	9	61	22G2	
Uxbridge (High Street)— Denham	GW	GW	1	9	39	5A2	2
Uxbridge (Vine Street)— West Drayton & Yiewsley	WR	GW	10	9	62	5A2	

1. *1.6.64.   **2.** Cl. 1.1.17 RO 1.5.19.   *24.2.64.

Station or line	Ownership at Closure	Pre-Group Company	Date Closed			Map Ref	Note
Velvet Hall	NER	NE	4	7	55	31D3	
Ventnor (West)—Merstone	SR	IWC	15	9	52	4G3	*
Victoria Park (NL platforms)	LMS	NL	8	11	43	40B3	
Victoria Park (GE platforms)	LNE	GE	1	11	42	40B3	

Station or line	Ownership at Closure	Pre-Group Company	Date Closed			Map Ref	Note
Waddesdon	MGC	MGC	6	7	37	10E2	1
Waddington	ER	GN	10	9	62	16B1	
Wadsley Bridge	ER	GC	15	6	59	42G2	
Wainfelin Halt	GW	—	5	5	41	43A2✠	
Waleswood	ER	GC	7	3	55	41A3	
Walkeringham	ER	GN&GE	2	2	59	22G5	
Wall	NER	NB	19	9	55	27B3	
Wallingford—Cholsey & Moulsford	WR	GW	15	6	59	10F3	

Station or line	Ownership at Closure	Pre-Group Company	Date Closed			Map Ref	Note
Walsall (Ryecroft Jn)— **Wolverhampton (HL)** (Heath Town Jn)	LMS	Mid.	5	1	31	15F4	
Walsden	LMR	LY	7	8	61	21E1	
Waltham	ER	GN	11	9	61	22F2	
Walton	NER	Mid.	12	6	61	42C2	9
Walton	ER	Mid.	7	12	53	17F2	
Wamphray	ScR	Cal.	13	6	60	26A3	
Wanlockhead—Elvanfoot	LMS	Cal.	2	1	39	30F4	*
Wansford	ER	LNW	1	7	57	17F1	
Wantage—Wantage Road	WT	WT	1	8	25	10F5	2
Wardhouse	ScR	GNS	5	6	61	37E2	
Warkworth	NER	NE	15	9	58	31F5	
Warrington (Arpley)	LMR	LNW	15	9	58	45D4	
Warthill	NER	NE	5	1	59	21C5	
Washingboro'	LNE	GN	29	7	40	17B1	
Washington	NER	NE	9	9	63	28C5	
Waterhouses—Durham (Dearness Valley Jn)	NER	NE	29	10	51	27D5	
Waterhouses—Leek (Leek Brook North Jn)	LMS	NS	30	9	35	15C4	13
Waterloo Road	LMS	NS	4	10	43	15C3	
Wath—Kirk Smeaton (Wrangbrook Jn)	LNE	HB	6	4	29	21F4	12
Watlington—Princes **Risborough**	WR	GW	1	7	57	10F3	3
Watten	ScR	HR	13	6	60	38D2	
Waverton	LMR	LNW	15	6	59	20E3	
Wavertree	LMR	LNW	5	8	58	45F4	
Wearhead—Etherley (Wear Valley Jn)	NER	NE	29	6	53	27D3	4
Wear Valley Junction	LNE	NE	8	7	35	27E5	
Weaste	LMS	LNW	19	10	42	45B3	
Weaverthorpe	LNE	NE	22	9	30	22A4	
Weedon	LMR	LNW	15	9	58	10B3	
Weelsby Road Halt	LNE	GN	10	3	52	22F2	5
Welbury	NER	NE	20	9	54	28F5	
Welton	LMR	LNW	7	7	58	10B3	
Wendlebury Halt	LMS	LNW	25	10	26	10D4	
Wentworth	ER	Mid.	2	11	59	42F2	
West Bay—Bridport	GW	GW	22	9	30	3F1	6
Westbury-on-Severn Halt	WR	—	10	8	59	8A1✠	
Westbury (Salop)	WR	SWP	12	9	60	14A1	
West Cults	LNE	GNS	5	4	37	37G4	
Westerham—Dunton Green	SR	SEC	30	10	61	5C4	*
Westhead Halt	LMR	LY	18	6	51	45E2	
Weston (Bath)	WR	Mid.	21	9	53	3A3	
Weston Rhyn	WR	—	12	9	60	20F4✠	
Weston & Ingestre	LMS	NS	6	1	47	15D4	
Weston-Sub-Edge Halt	WR	GW	7	3	60	9C5	
West Wemyss	ScR	NB	7	11	49	30A2	
Westwood	LNE	GC	28	10	40	42F2	

Station or line	Ownership at Closure	Pre-Group Company	Date Closed			Map Ref	Note
West Wycombe	WR	GW&GC	3	11	58	10F2	
Wheelock—Harecastle							
(Lawton Jn)	LMS	NS	28	7	30	15B3	
Whetstone	LMR	GC	4	3	63	16F4	
Whifflet	LNE	NB	22	9	30	44B3	
Whifflet (Lower)	ScR	Cal.	5	11	62	44B3	
Whippingham	SR	IWC	21	9	53	4F3	
Whipton Bridge Halt	SRy	LSW	1	1	23	2B3⚔	
Whissendine	LMR	Mid.	3	10	55	16E2	
Whitby (West Cliff)	NER	BM	12	6	61	28F2	
Whiteborough	LMS	Md.	4	10	26	41D3	
White Hart Halt	WR	—	30	6	52	43B3⚔	
Whitehurst Halt	WR	GW	12	9	60	20F4	
Whiteinch (Victoria Park)—							
Jordanhill	ScR	NB	2	4	51	44F4	
Whithorn—Newton Stewart	ScR	PPW	25	9	50	25D4	
Whitlingham Junction	ER	GE	19	9	55	18F2	
Whitmore	LMR	LNW	4	2	52	20F1	
Whitstable Harbour—							
Canterbury (West)	SRy	SEC	1	1	31	6B3	7
Whittington	ER	Mid.	4	2	52	41B2	
Whittington (High Level)	WR	Cam.	4	1	60	20G4	
Whittington (Low Level)	WR	GW	12	9	60	20G4	
Whitton—Scunthorpe	LNE	GC	13	7	25	22E4	8
Widmerpool	LMR	Mid.	28	2	49	16D3	
Wilbraham Road	LMR	GC	7	7	58	45A3⚔	
Willaston	LMR	LNW	6	12	54	20E2	
Willersley Halt	WR	GW	7	3	60	9C5	
Willesden Junction (Main Line)	LMR	LNW	3	12	62	39C4	
Wilsontown—Auchengray							
(Wilsontown South Jn)	ScR	Cal.	10	9	51	30C4	14
Wilstrop Siding	LNE	NE	1	5	31	21C4	
Wilton (North)	SR	GW	19	9	55	3C5	
Winchcombe	WR	GW	7	3	60	9D4	
Wincobank	ER	Mid.	2	4	56	42G2	
Wingham—Shepherds Well	SR	EK	30	10	48	6C2	10
Winsford & Over—							
Cuddington (Winsford Jn)	CLC	CLC	1	1	31	20D2	
Winson Green	LMR	LNW	16	9	57	13C3	
Winterbourne	WR	GW	3	4	61	9G2	
Wirksworth—Duffield	LMR	Mid.	1	1	49	41E1	11
Wishaw (South)	ScR	Cal.	15	9	58	44A2	
Wishford	SR	GW	19	9	55	3C5	
Wistanstow Halt	WR	—	11	6	56	14C1⚔	
Withington	WR	GW	2	1	61	9C1	
Withington & West Didsbury	LMR	Mid.	3	7	61	45A3	
Wixford	LMR	Mid.	2	1	50	9B4	
Wolvercote Halt	LMS	LNW	25	10	26	10E4	
Wood Green (Old Bescot)	LMS	LNW	5	5	41	13A2	
Woodhouse Mill	ER	Mid.	21	9	53	42G1	
Woodkirk	LNE	GN	25	9	39	42B2	
Woodside	LNE	GNS	5	4	37	37F4	

Station or line	Ownership at Closure	Pre-Group Company	Date Closed			Map Ref	Note
Woodville Road Halt	WR	TV	15	9	58	43B4	
Woofferton	WR	S&H	31	7	61	9A1	
Woolaston	WR	GW	1	12	54	9F1	
Wootton	SR	IWC	21	9	53	4F3	
Wootton Broadmead Halt	LMS	LNW	5	5	41	10C1	
Wootton Pillinge Halt	LMS	LNW	5	5	41	11D1	
Workington Bridge	LMR	LNW	1	1	51	26E3	
Worleston	LMR	LNW	1	9	52	15B2	
Wormald Green	NER	NE	18	6	62	21B3	
Wortley	ER	GC	2	5	55	42F3	
Wotton	LMR	GC	7	12	53	10E3	
Wrangaton	WR	GW	2	3	59	2D5	
Wrea Green	LMR	PWY	26	6	61	24D4	
Wreay	LMS	LNW	16	8	43	26C1	
Wryde	ER	MGN	2	12	57	17F3	
Wyke & Norwood Green	NER	LY	21	9	53	42B4	
Wylam	NER	NE	5	7	54	27B5	
Wylye	SR	GW	19	9	55	3C5	
Wynnville Halt	WR	—	12	9	60	20F4✠	

1. Formerly Waddesdon Manor. **2.** *19.12.45. **3.** Watlington—Chinnor* 2.1.61. **4.** Wearhead—St. John's Chapel* 2.1.61. **5.** PC. TC 1.1.40. **6.** *3.12.62. **7.** *1.12.52 RO −.1.53 to −.7.53 for flood repair work. **8.** Whitton—West Halton* 1.10.51; West Halton—Winterton* 29.5.61. **9.** Formerly Sandal & Walton. **10.** Wingham—Eastry* 25.7.50; Eastry—Eythorne* 1.7.51. **11.** PC. TC 16.6.47. **12.** Wath—Moorhouse & South Elmsallø; Moorhouse & South Elmsall—Wrangbrook Jn* 1.10.63. **13.** Waterhouses—Caldon Jn* 1.3.43. **14.** *4.5.64.

Station or line	Ownership at Closure	Pre-Group Company	Date Closed			Map Ref	Note
Yarm	NER	NE	4	1	60	28F5	
Yarmouth (Beach) (Lowestoft Line Jn)**—Gorleston (North)**	ER	MGN	21	9	53	18F1	1
Yarmouth (Beach)—Peterborough (Wisbech Jn)	ER	MGN	2	3	59	18F1	2
Yarnton	WR	GW	18	6	62	10E4	
Yaxley & Farcet	ER	GN	6	4	59	11A2	
Yealmpton—Plymstock	GW	GW	6	10	47	2E5	3
Yeoveney	WR	—	14	5	62	5B1✠	
Yockleton Halt	WR	SWP	12	9	60	14A1	

1. Caister Road Jn—Gorleston North*. **2.** Wisbech North (Horse Shoe Lane Crossing)—South Lynn, East Rudham—Yarmouth (Beach)*; Eye Green (Dogsthorpe Sdg)—Wisbech Jn* 17.12.60. **3.** Cl. 7.7.30, RO 3.11.41, when service ran from Plymouth Friary SR.* 29.2.60.